CRUEL AND UNUSUAL PUNISHMENT WITHIN OUR PRISON SYSTEM

A Study of Cases and Treatises

By

ANANT KUMAR TRIPATI

Copyright © 2020

ISBN-13: 978-1-947170-23-0

All rights Reserved.

No part of this book may be reproduced or transmitted in any form by any means, graphic, electronic or mechanical including photocopying, recording, taping or by any information storage or retrieval system without written permission from publisher.

The purpose of this book is to inform, educate and entertain. Although every precaution has been taken in preparation of this book, there may be errors or omissions. Neither is any liability assumed for damages resulting, directly or indirectly, from the use of this information contained within this book.

Published by:
SureShot Books Publishing LLC
P.O. Box 924
Nyack, New York 10960
www.sureshotbooks.com

KEY WORDS

Denying the indigent equality of arms principled sentencing what is an excessive sentence consecutive sentences retroactivity

Anant Kumar Tripati

ABSTRACT

This book looks into how the US Prison systems imposes penalties and punishment on those who it prosecutes and shows why the system violates ICCPR in ALL 52 states.

Anant Kumar Tripati

TABLE OF CONTENTS

KEY WORDS iii

ABSTRACT v

TABLE OF CONTENTS vii

ABOUT THE PAPER.. xi

DENYING THE INDIGENT EQUALITY OF ARMS SO AS TO ENSURE THEY ARE IMPRISONED VIOLATES ICCPR 1

    John D. King, Lamentations, Celebrations, and Innovations: Gideon at 50, 70 Wash. & Lee L. Rev. 835 (2013).............................. 1

PRINCIPLED SENTENCING: WHAT IS AN EXCESSIVE SENTENCE 3

    Cruel and Unusual | U.S. Sentencing Practices in a Global Context Professor Connie de la Vega Amanda Solter Soo-Ryun Kwon Dana Marie Isaac May 2012 3

CONSECUTIVE SENTENCES 13

HOW IT BECAME POSSIBLE FOR SOMEONE TO BE SENTENCED TO LIFE WITHOUT PAROLE FOR A NONVIOLENT OFFENSE... 24

STATES THAT SENTENCE INDIVIDUALS TO LIFE WITHOUT THE POSSIBILITY OF PAROLE FOR NONVIOLENT OFFENSES.. 26

THE CURRENT SWING AGAINST NONVIOLENT LIFE WITHOUT PAROLE SENTENCES 29

CHOOSING THE APPROPRIATE EIGHTH AMENDMENT DOCTRINE: THE GROSS DISPROPORTIONALITY APPROACH OR THE CATEGORICAL APPROACH?... 33

EVALUATING THE CASE FOR AN EIGHTH AMENDMENT CATEGORICAL BAN OF LIFE WITHOUT THE POSSIBILITY OF PAROLE SENTENCE FOR INDIVIDUALS CONVICTED OF NONVIOLENT OFFENSES 52

Evaluating Objective Evidence of a National Consensus 52
The Number of Jurisdictions That Authorize the Punishment and the Number That Prohibit It 52

THE DIRECTION OF LEGISLATIVE CHANGE 57

THE NUMBER OF SENTENCES IMPOSED 61

THE DEGREE OF GEOGRAPHIC ISOLATION 69

SUMMARY OF THE NATIONAL CONSENSUS ANALYSIS 72

EVALUATING THE SUPREME COURT'S INDEPENDENT JUDGMENT 73

THE CULPABILITY OF THE OFFENDERS IN LIGHT OF THEIR CRIMES 74

THE SEVERITY OF THE PUNISHMENT IN QUESTION 77

THE VALIDITY OR INVALIDITY OF PENOLOGICAL GOALS 78

DETERRENCE 79

RETRIBUTION 82

REHABILITATION 84

INCAPACITATION 85

INTERNATIONAL OPINION 88

WHAT ACADEMIC 'S STATE 91

Consecutive Sentences as Defacto Life Sentences 91

THE EVOLVING STANDARDS OF DECENCY AND RETROACTIVITY 106

Cruel, Unusual, And Completely Backwards: An Argument Forretroactive Application Of The Eighth AmendmenT *
Copyright © 2015 by Nishi Kumar. J.D., 2015,
New York University School of Law; B.A., 2010, Columbia University. 107

WHAT IS RETROACTIVITY? 110

**REQUIREMENTS FOR FEDERAL HABEAS CORPUS RELIEF AND
SUCCESSIVE PETITIONS** 117

RETROACTIVITY IN EIGHTH AMENDMENT CASE LAW 120

EVOLVING STANDARDS OF DECENCY AND PROPORTIONALITY REVIEW 123

DIMINISHED STATE INTEREST IN FINALITY 135

THE NEW FRAMEWORK AND ITS PRACTICAL IMPLEMENTATION 144

    Norval Morris, Towards Principled Sentencing, 37 Md. L. Rev. 267 (1977) 146

**FAILURE OF FEDERAL AND STATE JUDGES IN ARIZONA TO BRING THE RULE
OF LAW TO SENTENCING ENCOURANGES VINDICTIVE LEGISLATION**............ 160

    John S. Martin, Jr., Cruel and Usual: Sentencing in the Federal Courts Jurist in Residence, 26 Pace L. Rev. 489 (2006) 160

    Peter A. Ozanne, Bringing the Rule of Law to Criminal Sentencing: Judicial Review, Sentencing Guidelines and a Policy of Just Deserts, 13 Loy. U. Chi. L. J. 721 (1982). 173

**DUE TO EXCESSIVE SENTENCES IMPOSED BY ARIZONA JUDGES --
EXCESSIVE WHEN COMPARAED TO THOSE IMPOSED BY THE FEDERAL
SYSTEM, OTHER STATES AND THE INTERNATIONAL COMMUNITY
MANDATES APPLYING THE EIGHTH AMENDMENT AND ICCPR**...................... 177

    Nancy Gertner, A Short History of American Sentencing: Too Little Law, Too Much Law, or Just Right, 100 J. Crim. L. & Criminology 691 (2010) 177

    Richard Frase, Excessive Prison Sentences, Punishment Goals, and the Eighth Amendment: "Proportionality" Relative To WHAT? 89 Minn. L. Rev. 571 (2005) 181

**MEANINGFUL PROPORTIONALITY REVIEW OF SENTENCES MUST BE
MANDATORY IN ARIZONA BY STATE AND FEDERAL JUDGES. THE EXCESSIVE
DEFERENCE TO LEGISLATURES WHO ENACTED VINDICTIVE PENALTIES
VIOLATES THE CRUEL AND UNUSUAL PROVISION AND ICCPR**...................... 191

    James J. Brennan, The Supreme Court's Excessive Deference to Legislative Bodies under Eighth Amendment Sentencing Review, 94 J.Crim. L. & Criminology 551 (2003-2004) 191

    Julian C. Jr. D'Esposito, Sentencing Disparity: Causes and Cures, 60 J. Crim. L. Criminology & Police Sci. 182 (1969).. 193

Paul J. Sullivan, Sentencing: Disparity, Inconsistency, and
a New Federal Criminal Code, 20 Cath. U. L. Rev. 748 (1971)..................... 199

Nancy Keir, Solem v. Helm: Extending Judicial Review under the Cruel
and Unusual Punishments Clause to Require "Proportionality" of Prison
Sentences, 33 Cath. U. L. Rev. 479 (1984).. 203

Allyn G. Heald, CRIMINAL LAW: United States v. Gonzales: In Search of a
Meaningful Proportionality Principle, 58 BROOK. L. Rev. 455 (1992)......... 205

EFFECTIVE APPLICATION OF CRUEL AND UNUSUAL PUNISHMENT IN ARIZONA MANDATES ALL SENTENCES BE REVISITED BY FEDERAL AND STATE COURTS..212

Louise S. McAlpin Harmelin v. Michigan: Effective Application of Anti-Drug Legislation or Cruel and Unusual Punishment? Nova Law Review Volume 16, Issue 3 1992 Article 14 212

VINDICTIVE PUNISHMENT IS THE ARIZONA NORM MANDATING REVIEW ...219

Jalila Jefferson-Bullock How Much Punishment Is Enough?: Embracing Uncertainty in Modern Sentencing Reform Journal of Law and Policy http://brooklynworks.brooklaw.edu/jlp Part of the Criminal Law Commons, Criminal Procedure Commons, Law Enforcement and Corrections Commons, Legislation Commons, and the Public Law and Legal Theory Commons 219

PORTIONING PUNISHMENT SHOULD BE REQUIRED IN ARIZONA AS THE PUNISHMENT IS CRUEL AND UNUSUAL AND DISPROPORATIONATE UNDER AMERICAN AND INTERNATIONAL STANDARDS 230

Nancyj. King Portioning Punishment: Constitutional Limits Onsuccessive and Excessive Penalties University of Pennsylvania Law Review [vol. 144:101.. 230

CONCLUSION 235

ABOUT THE PAPER

I do not use the traditional methods for writing law reviews in that I substantially quote from treatises to emphasize my point.

I look at the indigent being denied equality of arms so as to ensure they are imprisoned which violates ICCPR, principled sentencing discussing excessive sentences.

The paper then examines consecutive sentences, discussing how it became possible for someone to be sentenced to life without parole for a nonviolent offense. It looks at states that sentence individuals to life without the possibility of parole for nonviolent offenses.

The paper then examines The Current Swing against Nonviolent Life without Parole Sentences. It evaluates the Case for an Eighth Amendment Categorical Ban of Life without the Possibility of Parole Sentence for Individuals Convicted of Nonviolent Offenses by Evaluating Objective Evidence of a National Consensus

I then look at the direction of legislative change, the number of sentences imposed, and evaluate the supreme court's independent judgment.

The culpability of the offenders in light of their crimes, the severity of the punishment in question, the validity or invalidity of penological goals, deterrence, retribution, rehabilitation, incapacitation, international opinion are reviewed and discussed.

The paper then examines what academic's state, consecutive sentences as defacto life sentences, the evolving standards of decency and retroactivity, requirements for federal habeas corpus relief, successive petitions and vindictive legislation

It shows due to excessive sentences imposed by Arizona judges -- excessive when comparaed to those imposed by the federal system, other states and the international community mandates applying the eighth amendment and ICCPR. The paper then argues meaningful proportionality review of sentences must be mandatory in arizona by state and federal judges. The excessive deference to legislatures who enacted vindictive penalties violates the cruel and unusual provision and ICCPR.

The paper argues effective application of cruel and unusual punishment in Arizona mandates all sentences be revisited by federal and state courts and that portioning punshment should be required in arizona as the punishment is cruel and unusual and disproporationate under american and international standards.

DENYING THE INDIGENT EQUALITY OF ARMS SO AS TO ENSURE THEY ARE IMPRISONED VIOLATES ICCPR

"There can be no equal justice where the kind of trial a man gets depends on the amount of money he has." [1] .

John D. King, Lamentations, Celebrations, and Innovations: Gideon at 50, 70 Wash. & Lee L. Rev. 835 (2013)

The system is indeed broken. The Supreme Court's mandate that all states provide counsel to those accused of serious crime comes up today against the backdrop of scarcity among the states. When Gideon was decided, fewer than half of all criminal defendants were indigent; today, more than 80 percent are. A criminal justice system that incarcerated 217,283 people in 1963 today incarcerates approximately 2.3 million.4 The war on drugs has exacerbated already high levels of incarceration, with a particularly devastating impact on communities of color. As a result, states increasingly face higher rates of prosecution and correspondingly higher demands for indigent criminal defense.

---

[1] Griffin v. Illinois, 351 U.S. 12, 19 (1956).

As resources are inevitably spread thin, the promise and legacy of Gideon have suffered, in some cases significantly. The contributors to the Gideon symposium tackle head-on a variety of challenging issues with regard to Gideon's legacy and the rights to counsel today. How does a system fulfill its obligation to provide effective assistance of counsel when resources are so limited and political will is in short supply? To what extent, if at all, is triage an appropriate response to the practical difficulties of implementing the right to appointed counsel? Should we focus on preserving the core of Gideon's protections as opposed to expanding its scope? And what does the future hold for Gideon and its legacy?

PRINCIPLED SENTENCING: WHAT IS AN EXCESSIVE SENTENCE

Law and Global Justice

Cruel and Unusual I U.S. Sentencing Practices in a Global Context Professor Connie de la Vega Amanda Solter Soo-Ryun Kwon Dana Marie Isaac May 2012

"Our resources are misspent, our punishments too severe, our sentences too long." U.S. Supreme Court Justice Anthony Kennedy [2] U.S. law allows the same defendant to face prosecution twice, by both the federal and state government. [3] And even if legislators decide to enact laws that lighten sentences, the new law does not automatically apply to prisoners already serving their sentences. [4]

---

2 U.S. Supreme Court Justice Anthony Kennedy, Address at American Bar Association Annual Meeting (Aug. 9, 2003) (transcript available at http://www.abanow.org/2003/08/speech-by-justice-anthony-kennedy-at-aba-annual-meeting/).

3 Bartkus v. Illinois, 359 U.S. 121, 124, 128-129 (1959); Abbate v. United States, 359 U.S. 187 (1959).

4 1 U.S.C.A. § 109 (West 2012); S. David Mitchell, *In with the New, Out with the Old: Expanding the Scope of Retroactive Amelioration*, 37 Am. J. Crim. L. 1, 5 (2009).

The International Covenant on Civil and Political Rights, a human rights treaty that the United States has signed and ratified, says, "The penitentiary system shall comprise treatment of prisoners the essential aim of which shall be their reformation and social rehabilitation." [5] By ratifying this document, the United States has agreed that it will uphold this basic human right. Despite this obligation, the United States is an outlier among countries in its sentencing practices.

International law and practice indicate that when a change of law will benefit an offender it should apply retroactively. The majority of countries in the world (67%) provide for this type of retroactive application of ameliorative law. In contrast, the U.S. federal government and state legislatures frequently refuse to apply the lighter penalty to those already sentenced.[6]

Article 10(3) ICCPR provides that countries have the obligation to make prison systems provide "treatment of prisoners the essential aim of which shall be their reformation and social rehabilitation. Juvenile offenders shall be segregated from adults and be accorded

---

5 International Covenant on Civil and Political Rights, Dec. 16 1966, S. Treaty Doc. No. 95-20 (1992), art. 10(3), 999 U.N.T.S. 171.

11 Ashley Nellis & Ryan S. King, The Sentencing Project, No Exit: The Expanding Use of Life Sentences in America, (2009).

6 1 U.S.C.A. § 109 (West 2012); S. David Mitchell, *In with the New, Out with the Old: Expanding the Scope of Retroactive Amelioration*, 37 Am. J. Crim. L. 1, 5 (2009).

treatment appropriate to their age and legal status." The United States ratified the ICCPR in 1992.

"Among mainstream politicians and commentators in Western Europe, it is a truism that the criminal justice system of the United States is an inexplicable deformity." Vivien Stern, secretary general of Penal Reform International[7]

The issue is that American prison stays are on average much longer than in the rest of the world. [8] Sentence severity in the United States has reached an extreme that contradicts its stated human rights obligation to direct its prisons system towards the primary goals of reformation and social rehabilitation, as set forth in the International Covenant on Civil and Political Rights (ICCPR), which it ratified in 1992. Consecutive sentences which stack up to the equivalent of de facto life without parole sentences by breaking up conduct into separate crimes deprive prisoners of potential rehabilitation. Mandatory minimum sentences in particular for drug crimes, de-emphasize defendants' need for treatment and drug therapy and instead emphasize incapacitation and retribution.

---

[7] Adam Liptak, *Inmate Counts in U.S. Dwarfs Other Nations'*, N.Y. Times, Apr. 23, 2008,
http://www.nytimes.com/2008/04/23/us/23prison.html.

[8] For example, burglary convicts serve on average 16 months in prison in the United States, compared to five months in Canada or seven months in England. *Id.* (citing Marc Mauer, Executive Director of The Sentencing Project).

When the Supreme Court has ruled on the disproportionality of sentences other than capital punishment, its test has been whether a penalty is "grossly disproportionate," [9] in deference to legislatures and their "assessment of the efficacy of various criminal penalty schemes." The U.S. Supreme Court has taken into account international standards when ruling that particular sentences violate the Eighth Amendment's prohibition on "cruel and unusual punishments." [10] Indeed, the United States has a long tradition of incorporating international law into its own, starting from the country's founding. [11] In the first of a long line of cases citing international and foreign law, the Court stated that "civilized nations of the world are in virtual unanimity that statelessness [the

---

9 See Rummel v. Estelle, 445 U.S. 263 (1980) (allowing life with parole for obtaining money under false pretenses under a recidivist statute); Harmelin v.Michigan, 501 U.S. 957 (1991) (allowing life without parole for possession of cocaine); Ewing v. California, 538 U.S. 11 (2003) (allowing 25 years to life under a "three strikes" recidivism statute); Hutto v. Davis, 454 U.S. 370 (1982) (allowing forty years imprisonment for selling marijuana). See also, Solem v. Helm, 463 U.S. 277 (1983) (striking down LWOP for passing a worthless check); Youngjae Lee, *The Purposes of Punishment Test*, 23 Fed. Sent. Rep. 58 (2011). The proportionality analysis consists of two tests, the culpability test and the purposes of punishment test.

10 See Amnesty International, et al. as Amici Curiae Supporting Petitioners, Miller v. Alabama (2012) (No. 10-9646), 2012 WL 174238 for a more thorough treatment of the 8th Amendment jurisprudence citing international and foreign law and practice.

11 Amnesty International, et al. as Amici Curiae Supporting Petitioners, Miller v. Alabama (2012) (No. 10-9646), 2012 WL 174238.

punishment in question in the case] is not to be imposed as punishment." [12]

The United States, as party to the International Covenant on Civil and Political Rights, has agreed that its corrections system will be rehabilitative. [13] The treaty states that "[t]he penitentiary system shall comprise treatment of prisoners the essential aim of which shall be their reformation and social rehabilitation." [14]The Human Rights Committee, an independent body of experts that monitors implementation of the ICCPR by its states parties, wrote in its General Comment on Article 10 that "[n]o penitentiary system should be only retributory; it should essentially seek the reformation and social rehabilitation of the prisoner. States parties are invited to specify whether they have a system to provide assistance after release and to give information as to its success." [15]

While the United States differs from most countries in that it has both federal and state criminal jurisdictions, the U.S. Supreme Court has said that states must also carry out the United States' international legal obligations. [16] When ratifying the International

---

12 Trop v. Dulles, 356 U.S. 58, 102 (1958).
13 International Covenant on Civil and Political Rights, *art.* 10(3).
14 International Covenant on Civil and Political Rights, *art.* 10(3).
15 U.N. Human Rights Committee, *General Comment 21, art. 10,* 33, U.N. Doc. HRI/GEN/1/Rev.1 (1994).
16 Medellin v. Texas, 552 U.S. 491, 536 (2008) (Stevens, J. concurring): "One consequence of our form of government is that sometimes States must shoulder the primary responsibility for

Covenant on Civil and Political Rights, Congress wrote that "the United States understands that this Covenant shall be implemented by the Federal Government to the extent that it exercises legislative and judicial jurisdiction over the matters covered therein and otherwise by the state and local governments." [17] Thus, the country's international human rights treaty obligations extend to the states as well as to the federal government.

The Standard Minimum Rules for the Treatment of Prisoners, adopted by the United Nations as guidance, states that countries "should utilize all the remedial, educational, moral, spiritual and other forces and forms of assistance which are appropriate and available, and should seek to apply them according to the individual treatment needs of the prisoners. [18] The Basic Principles for the Treatment of Prisoners similarly provides that "favorable conditions

---

protecting the honor and integrity of the Nation." In a follow-up opinion on the denial of habeas corpus relief, Justice Stevens again emphasized the point: "I wrote separately to make clear my view that Texas retained the authority and, indeed, the duty as a matter of international law to remedy the potentially significant breach of the United States' treaty obligations . . ." Medellin v. Texas, 129 S.Ct. 360, 362, (2008) (Stevens, J., dissenting).

17 138 Cong. Rec. S4781 (daily ed. Apr. 2, 1992).

18 United Nations Standard Minimum Rules for the Treatment of Prisoners, adopted Aug. 30, 1955 by the First United Nations Congress on the Prevention of Crime and the Treatment of Offenders, U.N. Doc. A/CONF/611, annex I, E.S.C. res. 663C, 24 U.N. ESCOR Supp. (No. 1) at 11, U.N. Doc. E/3048 (1957), amended E.S.C. res. 2076, 62 U.N. ESCOR Supp. (No. 1) at 35, ¶ 56-59, U.N. Doc. E/5988 (1977).

shall be created for the reintegration of the ex-prisoner into society under the best possible conditions." [19] Regional human rights experts have agreed that long sentences can undermine the rehabilitative purposes of corrections. For example, the Special Rapporteur on Prisons and Conditions in Africa has stated, "Punishment which attacks the dignity and the integrity of the human being, such as long-term and life imprisonment...run contrary to the essence of imprisonment." [20]

The majority of countries in the world, 76% of nations with available information, have some type of enhanced penalties for habitual offenders or recidivists. Habitual offender laws provide for higher penalties based on previous criminal convictions and the individual's prior criminal history; offenders are punished for their past behavior in addition to their current crime. [21] Nonetheless, the severity and applicability of these sanctions differ wildly across jurisdictions. These sentences can be problematic when judicial discretion is removed and mandatory punishments are required regardless of the circumstances surrounding the offense. On the

---

19 Basic Principles for the Treatment of Prisoners, G.A. Res. 45/11, U.N. Doc. A/RES/45/111 (Dec. 14, 1990).
20 African Commission on Human and Peoples' Rights, *Report of the Special Rapporteur on Prisons and Conditions in Africa, Mission to the Republic of South Africa,* (June 14-30, 2004), *available at* http://www.achpr.org/english/Mission_reports/South%20Africa/Special%20Rap_Prisons_South%20Africa.pdf.
21 John Kimpflen, *Habitual Criminals and Subsequent Offenders,* 39 Am. Jur. 2d Habitual Criminals, Etc. § 1.

most extreme end of the spectrum, these laws may result in a sentence that is grossly disproportionate to the crime triggering the sentence. For instance, in certain jurisdictions in the United States, a person with past felony convictions may receive a harsher penalty for shoplifting than a first-time murder conviction. [22] This has helped create a system in which prisons are filling with repeat offenders serving extraordinarily long sentences for different offenses committed over a period of years. In California, roughly 24% of the total prison population is serving sentences for second and third strikes. [23] This means that a quarter of all California prisoners have received increased prison sentences due to prior convictions, without focusing on the severity of their most recent crime.

Generally, the decision to apply an enhanced penalty is made by a judge during sentencing. In some countries the recidivism statutes do not increase the actual prescribed penalty for the offense, but

---

22 See Lockyer v. Andrade, 538 U.S. 63 (2003) (in two separate incidences, Leandro Andrade stole a total of nine videotapes worth roughly $150 from a Kmart. Because he had previous felony convictions (all nonviolent), he received two consecutive terms of 25 years to life); Cal. Penal § 190(a) (West2012) (under the California Penal Code a defendant guilty of 2nd degree murder shall serve 15 years to life).

23 Cal. Dep't of Corr. and Rehab., Corrections: Year at a Glance 24 (Fall 2011), *available at* http://www.cdcr.ca.gov/News/docs/2011_Annual_Report_FINAL.pdf (As of December 31, 2010, 40,998 inmates of a total 162,821 were serving sentences for 2nd and 3rd strikes).

instead deem the habitual offender ineligible for parole for specified increments or the entire term of the sentence. In many countries, prior convictions may be considered an aggravating factor at sentencing. [24] Other statutes require a mandatory minimum sentence upon conviction of a second or third felony crime. In the United States this includes "three strikes and you're out" provisions which typically provide a sentence of 25 years to life for someone upon conviction of their third felony.

The United States has a long history of enacting habitual offender laws. [25]However, a dramatic acceleration occurred in the 1990s when legislatures enacted habitual offender laws, specifically three strikes laws, in reaction to perceived increases in crime rates and threats to public safety. Twenty-four states and the federal government passed some version of a three strikes law between 1993 and 1995. [26]In enacting these laws, the goal was to limit judicial discretion and create a formulaic method to keep "career

---

24 See Appendix for details on Afghanistan, Andorra, Armenia, Azerbaijan, Bolivia, Bosnia and Herzegovina, Chile, Croatia, Democratic Republic of Korea, Denmark, Germany, Latvia, Marshall Islands, Micronesia, Nigeria, Palau, Serbia, Seychelles, Sierra Leone, Spain, Swaziland, Switzerland, The Former Yugoslav Republic of Macedonia, Turkey, and Ukraine.

25 Franklin E. Zimring, Gordon Hawkins & Sam Kamin, Punishment and Democracy: Three Strikes and You're Out in California 4 (Oxford University Press 2001).

26 Anne Goldin, *The California Three Strikes Law: A Violation of International Law and a Possible Impediment to Extradition*, 15 Sw. J. Int'l Law 327, 330 (2009).

criminals" off the streets. The reasoning was focused on retribution, incapacitation, and deterrence. These laws encapsulate the belief that someone who has committed previous crimes will continue to do so and that these "habitual offenders" should be removed from society in order to keep the public safe. In addition, legislators and the general public believe that the threat of harsh sentences will serve a deterrent effect. While the deterrent effects of recidivism statutes are debatable, there is clear indication that these sentences have played a role in increasing the U.S. prison population as part of the proliferation in "tough on crime" sentencing laws enacted in the past 30 years. 27

---

27 Marc Mauer, *Why are Tough on Crime Policies so Popular?* 11 Stan. L. & Pol'y Rev. 9 (1999).

CONSECUTIVE SENTENCES

When offenders commit multiple offenses, some countries issue consecutive or cumulative sentences, which are served one after the other. Others issue concurrent sentences, which are all served simultaneously, entitling the inmate to release after he or she has served the term of the longest sentence, or in other words merge the punishments for lesser offenses into the most serious one. Some countries allow both types of sentencing. Whether conduct constitutes one or several crimes brings into question whether a conviction can be entered for all the applicable offenses as well as whether the total amount of punishment should be increased. [28] Courts and legislatures must then decide when criminal acts should be treated as one offense or several.

The practice of multiplying charges and convictions for the same criminal act is potentially problematic for several reasons. It can result in duplicative penalties that lose sight of the fact that there has been only one transaction. In criminal law, these interests can be protected to some degree by good legislative draftsmanship,

---

[28] Carl-Friedrich Stuckenberg, *A Cure for Concursus Delictorum in International Criminal Law?* 16 Criminal Law Forum 361, 362 (2005).

deletion of duplicative criminal provisions, and being watchful of "legislative proliferation." Consecutive sentences can become de facto life without parole sentences when the possibility of parole is moved beyond the expected lifetime of the defendant, such as when sentences stack up to be many decades long or a defendant is issued multiple life sentences.[29]

A systemic problem in the United States is that courts have not understood double counting, that is punishing one wrong as if it were two or more, as a major issue. As a result, neither courts nor legislatures have offered comprehensive remedies. For example, a defendant who makes a single sale of narcotics can be handed three consecutive terms for violating three laws: sale of narcotics outside the original stamped package, sale of narcotics not pursuant to the appropriate Treasury order forms, and sale of narcotics known by the seller to have been[30] illegally imported. In another example, if a defendant deposits a check obtained by fraud, he can be found guilty of both the National Stolen Property Act as well as the mail fraud

---

[29] Daniel Engber, *Isn't One Life Sentence Enough?* Slate, Aug. 19, 2005, *available at*
http://www.slate.com/articles/news_and_politics/explainer/2005/08/isnt_one_life_sentence_enough.html (last visited Apr. 12, 2012). For example, Dennis Rader, sentenced to 10 consecutive life sentences for the murder of 10 people, will be eligible for parole after having served a minimum of 175 years.
[30] Gore v. United States, 357 U.S. 386 (1958).

statute. [31] A person who robs a bank can be consecutively sentenced for both entering a bank with intent to commit robbery and for robbery. [32] An accountant who doctors his account books to defraud the Internal Revenue Service can have his sentence enhanced twice: once for his use of a special skill and again for using sophisticated means to hide the crime. [33]

Defendants are commonly prosecuted for preparatory crimes, such as conspiracy to commit other crimes, as well as have their sentences enhanced for particular intent, such as under hate crime statutes. [34] The same wrong can be prosecuted as multiple offenses, resulting in decades- to centuries-long sentences for first-time non-violent offenders, sentences sometimes far surpassing those for murderers. There can be a tendency for such sentences serving symbolic functions in high-profile cases.

Daniel Enrique Guevara Vilca, 26, was sentenced to 154 years in prison in November 2011 for 454 counts of possessing child pornography. Each count represented one image. This sentence was longer than some for manslaughter, aggravated assault, child

---

31 Pereira v. United States, 347 U.S. 1 (1954). The federal statutes held to have been violated were 18 U.S.C. § 2314 (1952) and the mail fraud statute, 18 U.S.C.§ 1341.
32 Prince v. United States, 352 U.S. 322 (1957).
33 U.S. Sentencing Guidelines Manual, §§ 3B1.3 and 2T1.1(b)(2) (2010).
34 *See* Apprendi v. New Jersey, 120 S.Ct. 2348 (2010).

molestation, and rape of minors. [35]Sholam Weiss was convicted of 78 counts, including racketeering, money laundering and fraud charges, for stealing money from National Heritage Life Insurance and received 845 years in prison. [36] His projected release date is in 2754.

Norman Schmidt, charged with conspiracy to commit mail fraud, wire fraud, and securities fraud, as well as actual mail fraud, wire fraud, and securities fraud, was sentenced to 330 years. [37] In California, Rodrigo Caballero was convicted of three counts of attempted murder for shooting at three teens and wounding one when he was 16. [38] He was sentenced to 110 years to life for three consecutive life terms.

---

35 Jacob Carpenter, *East Naples Man's Life Sentence for Child Porn Too Harsh, Attorney Says*, Naples News, Nov. 3, 2011, http://www.naplesnews.com/news/2011/nov/03/east-naples-mans-life-sentence-child-porn-too-hars/.

36 William K. Rashbaum, *845 Years in Prison, If the Authorities Can Catch Him*, N. Y. Times, Mar. 9, 2000.

37 Press Release, U.S. Attorney's Office, District of Colorado, Norman Schmidt Sentenced to 330 Years in Federal Prison for Multi-Million Dollar "High Yield" Investment Fraud, *available at* http://www.justice.gov/usao/co/press_releases/archive/2008/April08/4_29_08.html (last accessed Feb. 23, 2012).

38 Bob Egelko, *Court: Teen's 110-year Sentence is Constitutional*, SFGate, Jan. 19, 2011, *available at* http://www.sfgate.com/cgi-bin/article.cgi?f=/c/a/2011/01/18/BA2R1HAT4J.DTL

He will be eligible for parole in 2112, when he is 122 years old.[39] He is therefore effectively sentenced to die in prison.

U.S. state and federal courts have repeatedly rejected claims that consecutive sentences constitute cruel and unusual punishment. [40] Courts have permitted 20 years imprisonment (two consecutive 10-year sentences) for passing bad checks [41] and 30 years for wire fraud (six consecutive 5-year sentences), sentences which in other countries are reserved for violent crimes. [42]

Historically, in common law, judges were entrusted with the decision whether sentences for discrete offenses should be served consecutively or concurrently. [43] Under U.S. federal law, federal courts can issue concurrent and consecutive sentences. Similarly, many states have enacted statutes or rules of criminal procedure or courts have issued case decisions to allow consecutive sentencing. [44] Some states establish a presumption of consecutive sentences

---

39 Brief for Appellant at 1, California v. Rodrigo Caballero, No. B217709 (2nd App. District Div. 4, 2011).
40 *See generally*, Howard J. Halperin, *Length of Sentence as Violation of Constitutional Provisions Prohibiting Cruel and Unusual Punishment,* 33 A.L.R. 3d 335(1970).
41 Boerngen v. U.S., 326 F.2d 326 (5th Cir. 1964).
42 Lindsey v. U.S., 332 F.2d 688 (9th Cir. 1964).
43 Oregon v. Ice, 555 U.S. 160 (2009).
44 Erin E. Goffette, Note, *Sovereignty in Sentencing: Concurrent and Consecutive Sentencing of a Defendant Subject to Simultaneous State and Federal Jurisdiction,* 37 Val. U. L. Rev. 1035, 1050, FN 67 (2003); *See* Alexander Bunin, *Time and Again:*

with concurrent sentences issued only when the court explicitly lists its reasons for issuing its sentences simultaneously. [45] Some state laws require consecutive sentencing for certain crimes, such as crimes committed by a prisoner or escapee, sex offenses, other offenses committed while in possession of a firearm, or multiple offenses of the same statute. [46]

There has been little principled consistency in the United States as to whether sentences should run concurrently or consecutively. [47]

Concurrent and Consecutive Sentences Among State and Federal Jurisdictions, Champion 34, Mar. 21, 1997.

45 249 These include Delaware, D.C., Florida, Louisiana, Montana, Virginia, Washington, West Virginia, and Wyoming. See, e.g., Del. Code Ann. tit. 11, § 3901(d) (West 2012) (ordering that no term of imprisonment for a state offense shall be run concurrently with any other state sentence); D.C. Code Ann. § 23-112 (West 1996); Fla. Stat. Ann. § 921.16(1) (West 2012); La. Code Crim. Proc. Ann. art. 883 (West 2012) (mandating a presumption of consecutive sentences under specific conditions); Mont. Code Ann. § 46- 18-401(1)(a), (4) (West 2001); Va. Code Ann. § 19.2-308 (Michie 2000); Wash. Rev. Code Ann. § 9.92.080(3) (West 2012); W. VA. CODE § 61-11-21 (West 2000); see also Robertson v. Superintendent of Wise Corr. Unit, 445 S.E.2d 116, 117 (Va. 1994); Keith v. Leverette, 254 S.E.2d 700, 703 (W. Va. 1979); Apodaca v. State, 891P.2d 83, 85 (Wyo. 1995). See Brief of the National Association of Criminal Defense Lawyers as Amicus Curiae in Support of Respondent, Oregon v. Ice, 555 U.S. 160 (2009) (No. 07-901), 2008 WL 3539502, for comprehensive coverage of states' consecutive sentencing statutes.

46 Erin E. Goffette, Note, Sovereignty in Sentencing: Concurrent and Consecutive Sentencing of a Defendant Subject to Simultaneous State and Federal Jurisdiction, 37 Val. U. L. Rev. 1035, 1050, FN 71 (2003).

47 See 24 C.J.S. Criminal Law § 2098.

As a result, there is an array of tests to assess whether two crimes are the same or not. The wide discretion given to judges and the multitude of legal tests to distinguish whether an act comprises more than one crime indicate that the problem of multiple offenses is one that has invited diverse judicial approaches that sometimes allow consecutive sentences and sometimes do not. [48]

The "Blockburger test" from Blockburger v. United States says that offenses are different if each requires proof of some fact that the other does not. [49] This test merges lesser included offenses, like robbery, into their aggravated versions, such as armed robbery because a robbery conviction needs no further proof than that required for armed robbery. The U.S. Sentencing Commission's Sentencing Guidelines acknowledges this need to avoid redundant counts by sorting greater and lesser included crimes. [50]

The statute states, "If multiple terms of imprisonment are imposed on a defendant at the same time, or if a term of imprisonment is imposed on a defendant who is already subject to an undischarged

---

48 See Phillip E. Johnson, Multiple Punishment and Consecutive Sentences: Reflections on the Neal Doctrine, 59 Cal. L. Rev. 357 (1970).
49 Blockburger v. U.S., 284 U.S. 299 (1932). Though the Blockburger test is often referenced with respect to double jeopardy, it is also used to distinguish whether the same act has constituted more than one crime, such as in the issuance of multiple sentences.
50 U.S. Sentencing Guidelines Manual, § 3D1.2 n.3 (2010).

term of imprisonment, the terms may run concurrently or consecutively, except that the terms may not run consecutively for an attempt and for another offense that was the sole objective of the attempt. Multiple terms of imprisonment imposed at the same time run concurrently unless the court orders or the statute mandates that the terms are to run consecutively. Multiple terms of imprisonment imposed at different times run consecutively unless the court orders that the terms are to run concurrently."

The "same act or transaction" test, advocated by U.S. Supreme Court Justice William Brennan in several dissenting opinions, treats two offenses as the same if they arise from the same course of conduct, no matter how many crimes a prosecutor could allege and no matter the definitional differences between them. [51] While the Supreme Court has not adopted this test, 17 states have in order to ban successive prosecutions. [52]

---

[51] State v. Truitt, 454 U.S. 1047 (1981) (Brennan, J., concurring); Ashe v. Swenson, 397 U.S. 436, 453 (1970) (Brennan, J., concurring); Brooks v. Oklahoma, 456 U.S. 999, 1000 (1982) (Brennan, J., dissenting); Snell v. United States, 450 U.S. 957, 958 (1982) (Brennan, J., dissenting); Werneth v. Idaho, 449 U.S. 1129, 1130 (1981)(Brennan, J., dissenting) (joined by Marshall, J.); Duncan v. Tennessee, 405 U.S. 127, 131 (1972) (Brennan, J., dissenting) (joined by Douglas, J., Marshall, J.).

[52] George C. Thomas III, The Prohibition of Successive Prosecutions for the Same Offense: In Search of a Prohibition, 71 Iowa L. Rev. 323, 376 (1986) (describing range of "same offense" test

Several state courts use a "single intent" test; if they were animated by a single criminal purpose, offenses are the same. This prevents cumulative punishment when the same conduct violates multiple laws or is difficult to break into units for prosecution. [53] With the proliferation of laws at both state and federal levels in the United States, a broad range of conduct has become criminalized. [54] The explosion of federal law creating over 4,000 crimes means that federal prosecution is possible at the same time state prosecution is, which sometimes means that sentences must be served consecutively in first a federal prison and then a state prison, or vice versa. [55]

In 2010, the Supreme Court issued a unanimous decision that a federal gun statute [56] tacking on an extra mandatory minimum of

---

[53] Rough Justice in America, Too Many Law, Too Many Prisoners, The Economist, Jul. 22, 2010, http://www.economist.com/node/16636027 (last accessed Apr. 9, 2012). Criminalized conduct includes "interstate transport of water hyacinths, trafficking in unlicensed dentures, or misappropriating the likeness of Woodsy Owl.

[54] See Note, Erin E. Goffette, Sovereignty in Sentencing: Concurrent and Consecutive Sentencing of a Defendant Subject to Simultaneous State and Federal Jurisdiction, 37 Val. U. L. Rev. 1035 (2003); Rough Justice in America, Too Many Law, Too Many Prisoners, The Economist, Jul. 22, 2010.

[55] Setser v. United States (No. 10-7387) http://www.scotusblog.com/case-files/cases/setser-v-united-states/. See Alexander Bunin, Time and Again: Concurrent and Consecutive Sentences Among State and Federal Jurisdictions, Champion 34 (Mar. 21, 1997).

[56] Crim. Pro. Code, 18 U.S.C. § 924(c).

five years for gun possession, seven years for blandishment, or 10 years for discharge for persons convicted of a drug or violent crime was permissible.[57] The decision confirmed that such sentences are not only mandatory minimums, but also consecutive, so that they must be imposed in addition to any other sentence, including the sentence for the underlying drug offense or other crime of violence.[58] Prosecutors can effectively seek an additional five-year sentence for mere gun possession at the same time of the commission of a crime, even if the gun was not used in the commission of the crime. The issuance of consecutive sentences, particularly when paired with mandatory minimums can result in de facto life imprisonment sentences. Consecutive sentences amounting to life or near-life sentences, particularly for non-violent offenses such as selling drugs prioritize retributive interests. Most importantly, such sentences neglect the possibility that offenders can be rehabilitated.

Weldon Angelo's, a then 24-year-old music producer in Utah with no prior convictions, was sentenced in federal court for three related marijuana sales of about $350 each. Since he possessed a weapon during the course of these sales, the sentencing judge was required to impose harsh consecutive penalties, regardless of the fact that the

---

57 Abbott v. Gould, 131 S. Ct. 18 (2010).

58 Abbott v. Gould, 131 S. Ct. 18 (2010); U.S. Supreme Court Rules Against Abbott and Gould, Families Against Mandatory Minimums, http://www.famm.org/courts/FAMMLegalBriefs/USSupremeCourtrulesagainstAbbottandGould.aspx (last visited Apr. 13, 2012).

gun was never used in the sales. Angelo's is currently serving a 55-year sentence with no possibility of parole during that time in federal prison. [59]

Bidish J. Sarma and Sophie Cull[60], write:

As[61] the nation moves away from the policies that built a criminal justice system bent on mass incarceration, it is an appropriate time to reassess a sentencing regime that has doomed thousands of individuals convicted of nonviolent offenses to die in prison. Over the last thirty years, those policies have resulted in more than 3,000 offenders across the country receiving life sentences without the possibility of parole when they were convicted of a nonviolent crime. While it seems clear to many today that this harsh punishment is inappropriate for offenses that involved no physical harm to other people, the individuals serving these sentences continue to face life and death in prison. The Eighth Amendment offers these offenders an opportunity to demonstrate the unconstitutionality of their punishment to the Supreme Court—the institution in the best position to redress these excessive sentences of a bygone era.

---

59 Weldon Angelo's, Families Against Mandatory Minimums, http://www.famm.org/facesofFAMM/FederalProfiles/WeldonAngelos.aspx (last visited Apr. 9, 2012).
60 *The Emerging Eighth Amendment Consensus Against Life Without Parole Sentences for Nonviolent Offenses*, 66 Case W. Res. L. Rev. 525 (2015)
61 I have modified the text for emphasis

HOW IT BECAME POSSIBLE FOR SOMEONE TO BE SENTENCED TO LIFE WITHOUT PAROLE FOR A NONVIOLENT OFFENSE

The 1980s and 1990s saw the United States transform into the world's most carceral society,[62] in large part due to the dramatic expansion of state and federal government sentencing policies that imposed stiff mandatory minimum penalties for drug offenses and crippled the use of parole.[63] Among the millions of people that have subsequently been caught in the net of mass incarceration is a group of offenders sentenced to die in prison for nonviolent crimes. Just over 3,000 people are currently serving life without the possibility of parole sentences in the United States for

---

[62] *See generally* Michelle Alexander, The New Jim Crow: Mass Incarceration in the Age of Colorblindness (2010) (describing how U.S. policies, including the "War on Drugs," increased incarceration rates).

[63] *See, e.g.*, William J. Sabol et al., Urban Inst. Justice Policy Ctr.,The Influences of Truth-in-Sentencing Reforms on Changes in States' Sentencing Practices and Prison Populations (2002), http://www.urban.org/research/publication/influences-truth-sentencingreforms-changes-states-sentencing-practices-and-prison-populations/view/ full report [http://perma.cc/8D6A-2N6X] (analyzing in-depth the effects of sentencing policies in various states).

crimes that did not involve an act of violence.[4] these people are serving their sentences for property crimes, drug offenses, financial crimes, or public-order offenses.[5]

The number of people serving life without parole sentences for nonviolent offenses began to climb in the late 1980s when mandatory minimums for drug and gun offenses gained currency and parole was largely abolished in the federal system.[6] The vast majority of people serving life without parole for nonviolent offenses in 2012 were sentenced in the federal system: 2,074 of 3,278 nationally or sixty-three percent.[7]

This Article relies heavily on a groundbreaking report that the American Civil Liberties Union (ACLU) published in November of 2013. The report, titled "A Living Death: Life Without Parole for Nonviolent Offenses," provides a thorough factual assessment of the issue, including what jurisdictions utilize the punishment and how many offenders are under the sentence.[11] Although the factual information contained in the report was compiled more than two years ago, it remains the most comprehensive, reliable, and accurate publicly available source.

STATES THAT SENTENCE INDIVIDUALS TO LIFE WITHOUT THE POSSIBILITY OF PAROLE FOR NONVIOLENT OFFENSES

Louisiana and Oklahoma have closely mirrored the federal system regarding which type of nonviolent offenses they tend to punish with life without parole sentences. Nonviolent drug offenders make up one hundred percent of nonviolent prisoners serving life without parole in Oklahoma and eighty percent of nonviolent lifers in Louisiana. Like the federal government, both states give mandatory life without parole sentences to people convicted of certain drug offenses for a third time.[64] Both states are among the highest users of nonviolent life without parole sentences, and their statutes make clear why. Louisiana, which, behind the federal government, holds the second highest number of people

---

[64] See La. Stat. Ann. § 15:529.1(A)(3)(b) (2015). Mandatory life sentences will be imposed for a third or subsequent conviction for any drug offense punishable by 10 years or more. Qualifying offenses include simple possession of any amount of any Schedule I substance or a 3rd or subsequent conviction for simple possession of any amount of marijuana, or manufacture or sale of any amount of any Schedule I or II substance. See also Okla. Stat. Ann. tit. 63 § 2-415(D)(3) (West 2015). Mandatory life sentences will be imposed

serving nonviolent life without parole at four hundred and twenty-nine sentences, mandates these sentences for a third or subsequent conviction for simple possession of any amount of marijuana and offenses as minor as purse-snatching.[65] Other states that provide for mandatory minimums of life without parole for repeat nonviolent drug offenders include Alabama, Georgia, and Illinois[66]. Additionally, Oklahoma allows discretionary life without parole sentences to be imposed for some first-time nonviolent drug offenders[67].

Notably, neither Florida nor Mississippi provide for mandatory life without parole sentences for repeat drug offenses (though they do allow them as a discretionary matter). Both states—along with Alabama [68]— mandate life without parole sentences for certain

---

65 *See* State v. Lindsey, 770 So. 2d 339, 347–48 (La. 2000) (Johnson, J., dissenting) (arguing that the defendant's sentence of life without the possibility of parole for purse-snatching was constitutionally excessive and grossly disproportionate under the Eighth Amendment). For further examples of offenses for which Louisiana mandates life without parole for repeat offenders, see La. Stat. Ann. §§ 15:529.1(A)(3)(b), 14:65.1, 14:62, 14:66 (2015) (detailing offenses for which Louisiana mandates life without parole for repeat offenders).

66 Caitlyn Lee Hall, Note, *Good Intentions: A National Survey of Life Sentences for Nonviolent Offenses*, 16 N.Y.U. J. Legis. & Pub. Pol'y 1101, 1212–13 (2013).

67 *See id.* at 1124 (citing Okla. Stat. Ann. tit. 63 § 2-509(D) (West 2015)) (allowing for discretionary life without parole sentences for converting marijuana to hashish).

68 *See* Ala. Code § 13A-12-231(1)(d), (2)(d) (2014) (stating that manufacture, sale, etc. of 10 kilograms or more of cocaine or

nonviolent *first-time* drug offenders[69].In Mississippi, a person convicted of possession with intent to sell two ounces of heroin would receive a mandatory sentence of life without parole, even if that person had no prior criminal history.[70]

The other two states that use nonviolent life without parole sentences with regularity emphasize property crimes over drug offenses. Alabama has 171 prisoners serving life without parole for nonviolent for a third or subsequent conviction for manufacture, sale, etc. of, e.g., 25 pounds or more of marijuana or 10 grams or more of heroin.

1,000 pounds or more of cannabis results in mandatory life without parole sentence).
[69] Fla. Stat. Ann. § 893.135(1)(b)(2), (1)(b)(3), (1)(c)(2), (1)(c)(3) (West 2015); Miss. Code Ann. § 41-29-139(f) (2015).
[70] Miss. Code Ann. § 41-29-139(f) (2015).

THE CURRENT SWING AGAINST NONVIOLENT LIFE WITHOUT PAROLE SENTENCES

The widespread implementation of mandatory minimums and habitual offender laws has led to a well-documented crisis in federal and state prisons with unprecedented overcrowding and rapidly aging prison populations.[71] Former overseers of these policies, including former president Bill Clinton, members of Congress from both sides of the aisle, and the current President, are now turning against such policies and calling for redress. Both promises of executive clemency and proposed federal legislation have the potential to significantly reduce the size of the federal nonviolent life without parole population but only if significant hurdles can be overcome.

Many of the key architects of the 1980s and 1990s tough-on-crime laws have since come to reject them as "overly broad" and

---

71 Ed Pilkington, *Bill Clinton: Mass Incarceration on My Watch 'Put Too Many People in Prison,'* The Guardian (April 28, 2015), http://www.theguardian.com/us-news/2015/apr/28/bill-clinton-calls-forend-mass-incarceration [http://perma.cc/68RG-TWDV].

"overdone" particularly with respect to nonviolent offenders.[72] As early as 2000, when he was nearing the end of his presidency, Bill Clinton acknowledged that the laws of the previous two decades had swept up far too many people convicted of nonviolent crimes. He told *Rolling Stone* magazine that "[w]e really needs a reexamination of our entire policy on imprisonment. . ... There are tons of people in prison who are nonviolent offenders—who have drug-related charges that are directly related to their own drug problems." In that same interview, Clinton said that possession of small amounts of marijuana should be decriminalized, that nonviolent offenders are serving sentences that are too long in many cases, and that mandatory minimums need to be reexamined. Clinton told the magazine, "I don't believe, by and large, in permanent lifetime penalties." Around the same time, public support for alternative sentences for nonviolent offenders, particularly drug offenders, was shown to have increased, and support for mandatory sentences had decreased since the 1990s

Since 1998 there has been a slow but steady rollback of mandatory minimum laws, particularly for nonviolent offenders. Families against Mandatory Minimums provides a comprehensive list of

---

72 Jann S. Wenner, *Bill Clinton: The Rolling Stone Interview,* Rolling Stone magazine (Dec. 28, 2000),
http://www.rollingstone.com/politics/news/therolling-stone-interview-bill-clinton-20001228#ixzz3iiD7Cnfq [http://perma.cc/Z2QM-WFVB].

states that have reformed mandatory minimum penalties, some of which allowed reduced sentences for thousands of people at a time.[73] Michigan began the trend in 1998 when it repealed mandatory life without parole sentences for certain drug offenses and applied the law retroactively.[74] It followed up with further repeals of mandatory minimums for drug offenses in 2003 and 2010.[75] In 2012, California voters overwhelmingly supported a proposition to amend the state's "three strikes" mandatory minimum law so that its application was restricted to serious or violent felonies. The law had previously mandated a life sentence for any third offense, even if it was minor and nonviolent. Georgia lawmakers passed a bill that extends parole eligibility to certain nonviolent drug offenders who are sentenced to a term of at least twelve years up to a life sentence who were not previously eligible for parole consideration.[1] Even Louisiana, which continues to imprison the largest portion of people serving nonviolent life sentences among the states, passed a law in 2012 to provide

---

[73] Families Against Mandatory Minimums, Recent State-Level Reforms to Mandatory Minimum Laws 1 (2013).

[74] *Success Stories,* Bureau of Justice Assistance, https://www.bja.gov/ programs/justice reinvestment/success_stories.html [http://perma.cc/697D-RF97] (last visited Oct. 13, 2015).

[75] *Justice Reinvestment Initiative,* Bureau of Justice Assistance, https://www.bja.gov/programs/justicereinvestment/index.html [http:// perma.cc/6YS6-ZY6W] (last visited Feb. 19, 2016).

prosecutors with the ability to waive mandatory minimums in the case of nonviolent offenses.

More broadly, many states are looking for ways to transform their expensive and punitive sentencing schemes so that they encourage diversion and rehabilitation. For example, twenty-seven have signed up for the U.S. Department of Justice's "Justice Reinvestment Initiative" to date. South Carolina, one of the program's "success stories," has reduced the portion of its prison population that were low-level, nonviolent offenders to thirty-seven percent where it had previously made up more than half. Current and former state governors are now regularly touting the importance of directing nonviolent offenders out of the system.

The broader sentencing schemes which gave rise to the regular use of nonviolent life without parole have steadily fallen out of favor. As a growing number of jurisdictions turn away from habitual offender laws and mandatory minimum penalties, life without parole sentences for nonviolent offenders are increasingly concentrated in just a handful of states and the federal system. In a new era of "smart" rather than "tough" justice, these sentences appear increasingly extreme and outdated.

CHOOSING THE APPROPRIATE EIGHTH AMENDMENT DOCTRINE: THE GROSS DISPROPORTIONALITY APPROACH OR THE CATEGORICAL APPROACH?

What legal recourse do offenders serving life without parole sentences have available to challenge the harshness of their punishment? In terms of available constitutional claims, it is the Eighth Amendment that protects individuals against cruel and unusual punishments inflicted by the government. Before looking at how offenders can lodge the optimal constitutional challenge to the practice of sentencing individuals convicted of nonviolent offenses to life without parole, this Article identifies the two different doctrinal approaches that the Supreme Court has used to evaluate claims that a defendant's punishment is unconstitutional under the Eighth Amendment. It then explains how and why one approach better accounts for the emerging developments that indicate that the practice may be falling out of favor.

One doctrinal approach, the "gross disproportionality" approach, traditionally describes Court's analysis of Eighth Amendment sentencing challenges in noncapital cases.[76] The other approach, the "categorical" approach, typically describes Eighth Amendment challenges to a particular punishment based on the offense or a characteristic of the offender[77]; the Court has utilized this approach almost exclusively in capital cases.[78]

According to the Court, "[t]he Eighth Amendment, which forbids cruel and unusual punishments, contains a 'narrow proportionality principle' that 'applies to noncapital sentences.'" [79] To enforce this narrow principle, the Court has utilized a three-part test—the gross disproportionality approach—to determine whether a particular defendant's noncapital sentence is unconstitutional:

---

76 *See, e.g.*, Vicki C. Jackson, *Constitutional Law in an Age of Proportionality*, 124 Yale L.J. 3094, 3185 (2015) (indicating the Supreme Court rarely reviews prison sentences in noncapital cases, but when it does so, it employs a "gross disproportionality" standard).

77 *See, e.g.*, Linda E. Carter, *The Evolution of Justice Kennedy's Eighth Amendment Jurisprudence on Categorical Bars in Capital Cases*, 44 McGeorge L. Rev. 229 (2013) (explaining categorical bars to the death penalty).

78 *See, e.g.*, Rachel E. Barkow, *The Court of Life and Death: The Two Tracks of Constitutional Sentencing Law and the Case for Uniformity*, 107 Mich. L. Rev. 1145, 1155 (2009) (noting cases where the Supreme Court has used the categorical approach to refuse to impose the death penalty.

79 *See* Harmelin, 501 U.S. at 1005 (Kennedy, J., concurring in part and concurring in judgment) (describing the outcomes in Solem v. Helm, 463 U.S. 277 (1983) and Weems v. United States, 217 U.S. 349 (1910)).

The first part of the test consists of a threshold that typically bars application of the second and third parts. The threshold requires a comparison of offense gravity and sentence severity, and a determination of whether this comparison reveals "gross disproportionality." The second and third parts call for an interjurisdictional review of sentences received within the state for more and less serious crimes, and an interjurisdictional review of sentences received in other states for the same crime. If the threshold is not met, then proportionality analysis ends. Only if the threshold is met do courts apply parts two and three.

If a court determines a sentence is grossly disproportionate and confirms its threshold finding through interjurisdictional and interjurisdictional comparisons, it will strike down that particular defendant's sentence.[80]

Alternatively, the Supreme Court employs the categorical approach "when evaluating a statutory punishment's constitutionality as applied either to a particular criminal offense or a particular class of offenders."[81] Long ago, the Court held that "[t]he [Eighth]

---

80 Donna H. Lee, *Resuscitating Proportionality in Noncapital Criminal Sentencing*, 40 Ariz. St. L.J. 527, 529 (2008) (citations omitted).
81 Trop v. Dulles, 356 U.S. 86, 101 (1958) (plurality opinion).

Amendment must draw its meaning from the evolving standards of decency that mark the progress of a maturing society."[82]

To decide whether those evolving standards mark a punishment as unconstitutional,

> [t]he Court first considers "objective indicia of society's standards, as expressed in legislative enactments and state practice" to determine whether there is a national consensus against the sentencing practice at issue. Next, guided by "the standards elaborated by controlling precedents and by the Court's own understanding and interpretation of the Eighth Amendment's text, history, meaning, and purpose," the Court must determine in the exercise of its own independent judgment whether the punishment in question violates the Constitution.[83]

Under this approach, when the Court determines a punishment is unconstitutional, it creates a categorical prohibition that exempts

---

[82] Bidish J. Sarma, *How* Hall v. Florida *Transforms the Supreme Court's Eighth Amendment Evolving Standards of Decency Analysis*, 62 UCLA L. Rev. Discourse 186, 192 (2014).

[83] Ewing v. California, 538 U.S. 11, 20 (2003) (quoting Harmelin v. Michigan, 501 U.S. 957, 996–97 (1991) (Kennedy, J., concurring in part and concurring in judgment)).

individuals convicted of certain crimes or belonging to a particular class of offenders from the challenged punishment.[84]

The gross disproportionality approach provides next to no space for individuals sentenced to life without the possibility of parole to challenge their punishment on Eighth Amendment grounds. The categorical approach is superior to the gross disproportionality approach for several reasons: the gross disproportionality approach is doctrinally incoherent; the Supreme Court has almost entirely sapped whatever potency the gross disproportionality approach may have once retained in theory (if it ever had any); the categorical approach provides a meaningful framework within which individuals sentenced to die in prison for minor or nonviolent offenses can situate their claims for constitutional relief; and the categorical approach provides for uniformity—a value that evades the gross disproportionality approach altogether. And although its earlier jurisprudence once suggested that all noncapital Eighth Amendment challenges would be subjected to review under the gross disproportionality test, the Supreme Court has recently

---

[84] *See, e.g.*, Scott K. Petersen, Note, *The Punishment Need Not Fit the Crime:* Harmelin v. Michigan *and the Eighth Amendment*, 20 Pepp. L. Rev. 747, 761 (1993) ("In the 1980 decision of *Rummel v. Estelle*, the Supreme Court retreated from its past decisions that incorporated a proportionality guarantee in the Eighth Amendment.").

clarified and deepened its commitment to the categorical approach even in the noncapital context. [85]

Among its prominent drawbacks, the gross disproportionality approach rests upon unstable jurisprudential foundations.[86] The test that until recently ostensibly governed claims that punishments in noncapital cases were cruel and unusual first appeared in Justice Kennedy's concurring opinion in *Harmelin* in 1991.[87] Confusion reigned even before *Harmelin* and well before the Court's own eventual, albeit tentative,[88] embrace of Justice Kennedy's

---

[85] See Steven Grossman, *Proportionality in Non-Capital Sentencing: The Supreme Court's Tortured Approach to Cruel and Unusual Punishment*, 84 Ky. L.J. 107, 107 (1996) ("The result of [a] series of flawed opinions from the Supreme Court is that the state of the law with respect to proportionality in sentencing is confused, and what law can be discerned rests on weak foundations.").

[86] See Youngjae Lee, *The Constitutional Right Against Excessive Punishment*, 91 Va. L. Rev. 677, 693 (2005) ("There was no majority opinion [in *Harmelin*], but the opinion that eventually came to assume the status of law was Justice Kennedy's concurring opinion . . . ."); see also id. at 693 n.79 (citing cases); see also Eva S. Nilsen, *Decency, Dignity, and Desert: Restoring Ideals of Humane Punishment to Constitutional Discourse*, 41 U.C. Davis L. Rev. 111, 149 n.199 (2007) (noting that courts have continued to apply Justice Kennedy's test from *Harmelin*).

[87] In 2003, a plurality of the Court indicated that "[t]he proportionality principles . . . distilled in Justice Kennedy's concurrence guide our application of the Eighth Amendment." Ewing v. California, 538 U.S. 11, at 23–24 (2003) (plurality opinion).

[88] Lockyer v. Andrade, 538 U.S. 63, 72 (2003); see also Sara Taylor, Commentary, *Unlocking the Gates of Desolation Row*, 59 UCLA L. Rev. 1810, 1815 (2012) ("Moreover, to the extent that the Court has used the Punishments Clause to review noncapital

concurring opinion. When he set forth the test, Justice Kennedy pointed out that "though our decisions recognize a proportionality principle, its precise contours are unclear." The Court's inconsistent articulation of the proportionality principle's scope and its repeated failure to use a consistent test for determining whether a sentence was disproportionate prompted it to admit that its "precedents in this area have not been a model of clarity. . .. Indeed, in determining whether a particular sentence for a term of years can violate the Eighth Amendment, we have not established a clear or consistent path for courts to follow."[89] Not once has a majority of justices in a self-contained opinion adopted the gross disproportionality test. Given the history of an approach that has, at best, developed in fits and starts,[90] it may be that the next time the justices return to the

---

sentences, it has not provided a clear doctrine for lower courts, plaintiffs, and attorneys to follow in dealing with challenges to noncapital sentences.").

[89] See Lee, , at 692–93 ("The key cases . . . sit uneasily with each other, and there is still much uncertainty about how the case law will eventually settle, especially given the rarity of majority opinions in this area.").

[90] See, e.g., Taylor, at 1819 (2012) ("One source of uncertainty is a consistent thread of pluralities, concurrences, and dissents that have pushed back against the presence of any proportionality requirement in the noncapital context, suggesting that the principle could lose the support of a majority of the Court in the future."); see also id. at 1815 ("In each of the rare cases in which the Court has confronted an Eighth Amendment challenge to a noncapital sentence, it has applied a different rubric for analyzing the gravity of the offense. While some of the modes of analysis vary only slightly, in other cases the approach is completely different from anything the Court has done in the past. As a result, it is not clear how a court will review a given noncapital

approach, they will inaugurate another doctrinal shift, return to an old and substantively different formulation of the test, or perhaps abandon the underlying proportionality principle altogether.

Not only is the gross disproportionality test unstable,[91] but it has also proven to be toothless. The case law is "sparse," but the outcomes in a pair of 2003 Supreme Court cases, *Ewing v. California*[92] and *Lockyer v. Andrade*,[93] make clear that efforts to challenge long prison terms under the gross disproportionality approach are likely to fail.[94] In *Ewing*, the Supreme Court upheld a defendant's sentence of twenty-five years to life under California's three-strikes regime in which "[t]he sentence-triggering criminal conduct consist[ed] of the theft of three golf clubs priced at a total of $1,197."[95] And in *Andrade*, the Court reversed a lower court's grant of habeas relief to a defendant whom was sentenced to two

---

sentence to determine if it is grossly disproportionate, making it exceedingly difficult for prisoners to bring successful claims.").

91 *See also* Graham v. Florida, 560 U.S. 48, 86 (2010) (Roberts, C.J., concurring) ("Our Court has struggled with whether and how to apply the Cruel and Unusual Punishments Clause to sentences for noncapital crimes.").

92 538 U.S. 11 (2003) (plurality opinion).

93 538 U.S. 63 (2003).

94 *See, e.g.*, Erwin Chemerinsky, *The Constitution and Punishment*, 56 Stan. L. Rev. 1049, 1059 (2004) ("In 2003, in *Ewing* and *Andrade*, the Court greatly weakened, if not almost eliminated, proportionality review, as applied to prison sentences.").

95 Ewing v. California, 538 U.S. 11, 35 (2003) (Breyer, J., dissenting).

consecutive twenty-five-to-life prison terms under California's three-strike law for the theft of nine videotapes valued at approximately $150. [96] These cases culminate in what one commentator has called the "enfeeblement of the Eighth Amendment's proportionality requirement."

Many legal scholars, litigants, and commentators have critiqued the gross disproportionality approach because it essentially commands courts to defer to legislatures and prosecutors, removing extremely harsh sentences from the Constitution's reach. The words of Professors Steiker and Steiker appropriately summarize these critiques: "The application of this . . . threshold requirement of gross disproportionality has proven to be an insurmountable hurdle for Eighth Amendment challenges to long prison terms."[97] In other words, unless one subscribes to the premise that the Constitution does not entail a proportionality principle—a stance that one current

---

96 *See* Lockyer v. Andrade, 538 U.S. 63, 66 (2003) (describing the appellate court's disposition).

97 Carol S. Steiker & Jordan M. Steiker, *Opening A Window or Building A Wall? The Effect of Eighth Amendment Death Penalty Law and Advocacy on Criminal Justice More Broadly*, 11 U. Pa. J. Const. L. 155, 186 (2008); *see also* Taylor, at 1835 ("The doctrine is so narrow and forbids only such extreme sentences that it allows relief in a vanishingly small number of cases and allows almost any sentence to pass constitutional muster. The combination of an extremely high doctrinal standard and an extremely deferential treatment of state decisions allows the Court to conclude that sentences that are extremely harsh in comparison to the crime committed—sentences that should be viewed as grossly disproportionate—do not violate the proportionality principle.").

Supreme Court justice defends[98]— the current situation is bleak. The Constitution itself promises that the government will not inflict cruel and unusual punishments on individuals, but the Court has essentially decided that no noncapital sentence will ever be deemed unconstitutional. Rather than acknowledge that it has failed to devise an enforceable remedy to protect the individual's Eighth Amendment right, the Court has instead determined that the right means so little that it may as well not exist.[99]

While it may seem that the jurisprudence forecloses a meaningful Eighth Amendment challenge to life without parole sentences for individuals convicted of nonviolent offenses, the Court's other approach, the categorical approach, provides an alternative well worth exploring. Before 2010, the Court only utilized this approach in death penalty cases. Then, in *Graham v. Florida*,[100] the Court

---

[98] *See Ewing*, 538 U.S. at 32 (Thomas, J., concurring in judgment) ("In my view, the Cruel and Unusual Punishments Clause of the Eighth Amendment contains no proportionality principle."). Justice Scalia, who recently passed away, shared Justice Thomas's view about proportionality. *See* Harmelin v. Michigan, 501 U.S. 957, 985 (1991) (Scalia, J., plurality opinion) (finding "that those who framed and approved the Federal Constitution chose . . . not to include within it the guarantee against disproportionate sentences").

[99] *See, e.g.*, Taylor, at 1816 ("The Court's failure to develop a meaningful Eighth Amendment doctrine in the noncapital context has left a doctrinal vacuum in which the Court's articulation of the proportionality test is . . . so weak that it fails to adequately limit unconstitutional sentences.").

[100] 560 U.S. 48 (2010).

struck down the practice of sentencing juvenile offenders to life without the possibility of parole for nonhomicide crimes.[101] The categorical prohibition in *Graham* demonstrates that the Court no longer confines the categorical approach to death penalty cases. Whether *Graham* presages an extension of the categorical analysis to a broad range of prison-term sentences (beyond undeniably harsh life without the possibility of parole sentences)[102] or instead a demarcation of the approach's outer boundary,[103] the precedent has been set for the sentence at issue here.

---

[101] *See* William W. Berry III, *More Different Than Life, Less Different Than Death: The Argument for According Life Without Parole Its Own Category of Heightened Review Under the Eighth Amendment After* Graham v. Florida, 71 Ohio St. L.J. 1109, 1111 (2010) ("The United States Supreme Court's application of the Eighth Amendment over the past fifty years has clearly divided capital and non-capital cases. This dual approach has rested on the Court's oft-repeated notion that 'death-is-different,' . . . ."); Graham v. Florida, 560 U.S. 48, 60 (2009) (noting that "previous cases" invoking the categorical approach "involved the death penalty"); at 61 ("The present case involves an issue the Court has not considered previously: a categorical challenge to a term-of-years sentence.").

[102] *See Graham*, 560 U.S. at 82 ("The Constitution prohibits the imposition of a life without parole sentence on a juvenile offender who did not commit homicide."); *see also* Berry III, at 1111–12 ("In *Graham*, the Court applied its 'evolving standards of decency' standard, heretofore reserved for capital cases, to hold that the Eighth Amendment prohibited states from sentencing juvenile offenders to life without parole for non-homicide crimes.").

[103] *See* Jackson, at 3188 ("Whether these cases [including *Graham*] foreshadow a broader willingness to take a harder look at the constitutional proportionality of noncapital sentences is uncertain."); Taylor, at 1817–18 (noting that the "*Graham*

In order for the Court to undertake the categorical approach, the party challenging a sentencing practice must claim that a government cannot subject to that particular sentence either a person convicted of "a type of crime" or a person who falls within "a class of individuals."[104] *Coker v. Georgia*[105] provides an example of the "type of crime" challenge.[106] In that case, the Court categorically prohibited all jurisdictions from sentencing to death an individual convicted of the crime of rape of an adult woman.[107] It found that the "sentence of death is . . . excessive punishment for the crime of rape and is therefore forbidden by the Eighth Amendment . . . ."[108] Examples of cases in which "a class of individuals" was exempted from a punishment include *Atkins v. Virginia*[109] and *Roper v.*

---

decision[] may suggest a new willingness to expand the Eighth Amendment doctrine").

104 Carter, at 234; *see also Graham*, 560 U.S. at 60 (explaining that "one [subset of categorical challenges] consider[s] the nature of the offense, the other consider[s] the characteristics of the offender").

105 433 U.S. 584 (1977) (plurality opinion)

106 *Id.* at 592 (exemplifying a "type of crime" challenge).

107 *See id.* The Court also later held that the death penalty is an unconstitutional punishment for the crime of child rape. *See* Kennedy v. Louisiana, 554 U.S. 407, 446–47 (2008).

108 *Coker*, 433 U.S. at 592.

109 *See* Atkins v. Virginia, 536 U.S. 304, 321 (2002) (holding that the Constitution restricts imposition of the death penalty on persons with intellectual disabilities).

Simmons.[110] In those cases, the Court prohibited jurisdictions from sentencing to death individuals with intellectual disabilities[111] and juvenile offenders (under the age of eighteen at the time of the crime)[112] respectively.

Categorical challenges to a punishment need not separate the "type of crime" and "class of individuals" categories. While the Court historically dealt with challenges involving one or the other, in *Graham*, the Court ruled on a claim that "implicate[d] a particular type of sentence as it applies to an entire class of offenders who have committed a range of crimes."[113] The petitioner successfully combined a claim involving a "class of individuals"—juvenile offenders—and a "type of crime"—all nonhomicide crimes.

---

110 *See* Roper v. Simmons, 543 U.S. 551, 578 (2005) (holding that the Constitution prohibits imposition of the death penalty on persons under the age of eighteen).

111 *See Atkins*, 536 U.S. at 321 (holding that "we therefore conclude that such punishment is excessive and that the Constitution 'places a substantive restriction on the State's power to take the life' of a mentally retarded offender"). The Court recently explained that although "previous opinions of this Court have employed the term 'mental retardation,'" the Court now "uses the term 'intellectual disability' to describe the identical phenomenon." Hall v. Florida, 134 S. Ct. 1986, 1990 (2014). For more information about *Hall*, see Sarma, at 201.

112 *See Simmons*, 543 U.S. at 578 (holding that the "Eighth and Fourteenth Amendments forbid imposition of the death penalty on offenders who were under the age of [eighteen] when their crimes were committed").

113 Graham v. Florida, 560 U.S. 48, 61 (2010).

A categorical challenge to life without the possibility of parole sentences for individuals convicted of nonviolent offenses represents a challenge based on the type of crime or "nature of the offense."[114] Put simply, the challenge asserts that because the offenses for which these individuals were sentenced to die in prison were not violent in nature, the Eighth Amendment prohibits this "second most severe [sentence] known to the law"[115]—and the most severe sentence possibly available for those crimes.[116] That the categorical approach is available means that the gross disproportionality approach can be bypassed altogether.

The mere availability of a categorical challenge, however, does not prove that the approach avoids the downsides that attend the gross disproportionality approach. Indeed, a great deal of ink has been spilled in critique of the categorical approach as well. But unlike the gross disproportionality approach, the categorical approach is not incoherent, unstable, and impotent.

---

[114] Harmelin v. Michigan, 501 U.S. 957, 996 (1991) (plurality opinion).

[115] *See* Kennedy v. Louisiana, 554 U.S. 407, 437 (2008) (holding the death penalty unconstitutional for nonhomicide offenses against individuals (excluding crimes like terrorism and espionage)).

[116] *See, e.g.*, Robert J. Smith, Bidish J. Sarma & Sophie Cull, *The Way the Court Gauges Consensus (and How to Do It Better)*, 35 Cardozo L. Rev. 2397, 2415–18 (2014) (canvassing the critiques of the categorical approach).

In terms of doctrinal coherence, the categorical approach is far better developed and much more stable than its counterpart. To start, only a plurality of justices has adopted the current formulation of the gross disproportionality test that Justice Kennedy crafted in *Harmelin* and Justice O'Connor utilized in *Ewing*.[117] By contrast, a majority of justices has repeatedly reaffirmed the Court's approach to identifying evolving standards of decency and exercising independent judgment of a punishment.[118] Not only does the categorical approach have multiple definite majority opinions establishing the Court's commitment to it, but it also has proven to be a stable doctrine over a number of cases spanning several years.[119] And, whereas litigants and courts lack clear guidance on

---

117 *See, e.g., Graham*, 560 U.S. at 61 (describing the Court's sentencing approach under categorical rules); Hall v. Florida, 134 S. Ct. 1986, 1993 (2014) (identifying standards of decency and using the Court's independent judgment to determine whether to impose the death penalty on people with intellectual disabilities).

118 *See, e.g.,* Atkins v. Virginia, 536 U.S. 304, 320 (2002); Kennedy v. Louisiana, 554 U.S. 407, 420 (2008); *Graham*, 560 U.S. at 60–61 (2010); *Hall*, 134 S. Ct. at 2002–03 (2014) (drawing on the categorical approach to determine the constitutionality of sentencing decisions); *see also* William W. Berry III, *Eighth Amendment Differentness*, 78 Mo. L. Rev. 1053, 1066 (2013) ("Beginning in 2002, the Court has narrowly decided five cases holding that the Eighth Amendment categorically prohibits a certain type of offender or offense from receiving a certain punishment."); *see also* Carter, at 246 ("Justice Kennedy's powerful opinions using and defending this test provide consistency and integrity to the Court's decisions in this area.").

119 *See* Lockyer v. Andrade, 538 U.S. 63, 72 (2003) ("Our cases exhibit a lack of clarity regarding what factors may indicate gross disproportionality."). 185. Smith, Sarma & Cull, at 2406.

how the gross disproportionality approach really applies,[120] "the Court has developed and applied an increasingly sophisticated form of the [categorical] analysis on more than a dozen occasions." Although one could certainly critique the Supreme Court's entire Eighth Amendment jurisprudence (including the fact that two separate approaches apply in different contexts),[121] there is no doubt that between the two approaches, the categorical approach is more well-established and more stable.

The categorical approach is also superior because it demonstrates a capacity to detect and strike down punishments that are cruel and unusual. On the other hand, the gross disproportionality approach guts the Eighth Amendment protection because "the Court has treated proportionality as essentially lacking enforceable content in

---

[120] Indeed, many have. *See, e.g.*, Tom Stacy, *Cleaning Up the Eighth Amendment Mess*, 14 Wm. & Mary Bill Rts. J. 475, 477 (2005) ("One would be hard pressed to identify any other area of constitutional law plagued by such confusion at its very roots."); John F. Stinneford, *The Original Meaning of "Unusual": The Eighth Amendment as a Bar to Cruel Innovation*, 102 Nw. U. L. Rev. 1739, 1740 (2008) ("The feeling that modern Eighth Amendment jurisprudence has gone off the rails has arisen, at least in part, from the wildly inconsistent rulings that have emanated from the Supreme Court over the past few decades . . . .").

[121] *See* Harmelin v. Michigan, 501 U.S. 957, 986 n.11 (1991) (plurality opinion); *id.* at 1018 (White, J., dissenting); Rummel v. Estelle, 445 U.S. 263, 274 n.11 (1980) (plurality opinion); *id.* at 288 (Powell, J., dissenting) (describing how disproportionate punishment offends the American justice system).

its modern cases concerning other [noncapital] punishments."[122] It is so weak that one might conclude the *only* viable claim of disproportionality would arise from a life sentence imposed on someone for a parking meter violation.[123] Because gross disproportionality enshrines nearly absolute deference to legislatures that adopt criminal sentencing laws,[124] the categorical

---

[122] *See generally* James J. Brennan, Note, *The Supreme Court's Excessive Deference to Legislative Bodies Under Eighth Amendment Sentencing Review*, 94 J. Crim. L. & Criminology 551 (2004) (arguing that the Supreme Court should take a more assertive role against legislation that favors excessive prison sentencing). Some commentators have equated the gross disproportionality test with the notoriously weak and deferential Fourteenth Amendment rational basis test. *See, e.g.*, Lee, at 741 ("The deferential nature of the *Ewing* Court's disjunctive theory renders the prohibition on excessive punishment probably only as strong as a rational basis inquiry would permit, which is not very strong at all."); Christopher J. DeClue, Comment, *Sugarcoating the Eighth Amendment: The Grossly Disproportionate Test Is Simply the Fourteenth Amendment Rational Basis Test in Disguise*, 41 Sw L. Rev. 533, 570 (2012) ("In 1993, Justice Stevens described the Fourteenth Amendment rational basis test as 'tantamount to no review at all.' It is time for the Court to accept that the grossly disproportionate test is no different, and, by doing so, the Court must admit that the grossly disproportionate test is simply a rational basis test in disguise.") (footnote omitted).

[123] *See* Solem v. Helm, 463 U.S. 277 (1983) (holding that a sentence to life imprisonment without possibility of parole was disproportionate to the defendant's relatively minor criminal offense); *see also* Berry III, at 1065 ("*Solem*, though, is an outlier in light of the Court's decisions [concerning] . . . similar cases of disproportional sentences in non-capital cases.").

[124] Graham v. Florida, 560 U.S. 48, 77 (2010) (contrasting the Court's categorical approach with the "case-specific gross disproportionality inquiry"); *see also* Ewing v. California, 538 U.S. 11, 52 (2003) (Breyer, J., dissenting) ("Application of the Eighth

approach actually represents a better mechanism to enforce and give some perceptible meaning to the Constitution's ban on cruel and unusual punishments. The fact that several challengers have persuaded the Court to strike down sentencing practices stands in stark contrast to the lone outlier case in which an individual prevailed on a claim of disproportionality.[125]

One other major comparative advantage of the categorical approach is that, by definition, it ensures that the Eighth Amendment will apply uniformly across the country. The gross disproportionality test requires individual judges to make case-specific Eighth Amendment determinations on a case-by-case basis. The categorical approach, on the other hand, empowers the U.S. Supreme Court to make binding determinations followed by all other courts. To the extent that uniformity is a key value in the context of constitutional interpretation, the categorical approach protects that value, and the gross disproportionality approach sacrifices it, at least in theory.

The inadequacies that plague the gross disproportionality approach render it an unsuitable vehicle for considering the claim that it is unconstitutional to sentence individuals convicted of nonviolent

---

Amendment to a sentence of a term of years requires a case-by-case approach.").

125 *See* Coker v. Georgia, 433 U.S. 584, 597 (1977) (plurality opinion) ("[T]he Constitution contemplates that in the end our own judgment will be brought to bear on the question of the acceptability of the [] penalty under the Eighth Amendment.").

offenses to life without the possibility of parole. Because the constitutional issue here provides a clear category upon which to base a categorical challenge and because the categorical approach is far better equipped to deal meaningfully with the emerging facts, the appropriate Eighth Amendment framework is clear. The questions that remain are whether the Supreme Court should find that a national consensus against the sentencing practice exists, and, if it does, whether it should also find in its independent judgment that the punishment is unconstitutional.

EVALUATING THE CASE FOR AN EIGHTH AMENDMENT CATEGORICAL BAN OF LIFE WITHOUT THE POSSIBILITY OF PAROLE SENTENCE FOR INDIVIDUALS CONVICTED OF NONVIOLENT OFFENSES

Evaluating Objective Evidence of a National Consensus

The Number of Jurisdictions That Authorize the Punishment and the Number That Prohibit It

As part of its consensus analysis, the Supreme Court has always considered the number of jurisdictions—counting all of the states and the federal government—that legislatively authorize the punishment. According to the Court, "the legislative judgment weighs heavily in ascertaining such standards."[126] The number of jurisdictions that prohibit a punishment is not necessarily an outcome-determinative factor, but it can "weigh[] very heavily" in favor of an Eighth Amendment prohibition, especially if the number reflects a vast majority.[127]

---

126 Smith, Sarma & Cull, at 2406.
127 Gregg v. Georgia, 428 U.S. 153, 175 (1976) (plurality opinion); *see also* Roper v. Simmons, 543 U.S. 551, 564 (2005)

At the time the ACLU published its report on life without parole sentences for nonviolent offenders, the federal government and "22 states permit[ted] LWOP sentences for certain nonviolent crimes."[128] In other words, twenty-eight states did not permit the punishment. Looking at the cases in which the Court has found a consensus against a punishment, they indicate that, given the numbers here, this factor does not weigh heavily in favor of striking down the punishment. For example, in *Coker*, Georgia was the only jurisdiction that permitted the challenged punishment.[129] In

---

(stating that "[t]he beginning point [of the Eighth Amendment analysis] is a review of objective indicia of consensus, as expressed in particular by the enactments of legislatures that have addressed the question"); Penry v. Lynaugh, 492 U.S. 302, 331 (1989) (indicating that the "clearest and most reliable objective evidence of contemporary values is the legislation enacted by the country's legislatures"), *abrogated by* Atkins v. Virginia, 536 U.S. 304, 312 (2002).

128 *See* Coker v. Georgia, 433 U.S. 595–96 (1977) (plurality opinion) ("The upshot is that Georgia is the sole jurisdiction in the United States at the present time that authorizes a sentence of death when the rape victim is an adult woman . . . . The current judgment with respect to the death penalty for rape is not wholly unanimous among state legislatures, but it obviously weighs very heavily on the side of rejecting capital punishment as a suitable penalty for raping an adult woman.").

129 *Coker*, 433 U.S. at 595–96 (plurality opinion). Turner & Bunting, at 23; *see also id.* at 39 (listing the jurisdictions that permit life without parole for certain nonviolent offenses: Alabama, Arizona, Arkansas, Delaware, Florida, Georgia, Illinois, Indiana, Iowa, Kentucky, Louisiana, Michigan, Mississippi, Missouri, Nevada, North Dakota, Oklahoma, South Carolina, South Dakota, Virginia, Wisconsin, Wyoming, and the federal government). This number is comparable to a determination of the number of states that permit life without parole for nonviolent offenses done in a 2013 law review Note. *See generally* Hall,

Kennedy, the Court found that forty-four states did not permit the challenged punishment.¹³⁰ Unlike *Kennedy* and *Coker*, the number of jurisdictions that prohibit life without parole for nonviolent offenses does not approach a level that demonstrates to the Court that legislatures have almost universally rejected the punishment.

While the count of twenty-eight does not compare as favorably to the head counts in *Coker* and *Kennedy*, in both *Atkins* and *Simmons* the Court found that thirty states disallowed the execution of members of the relevant class of offenders.¹³¹ And, in *Graham*, "the Court ultimately found a national consensus even though it tallied only thirteen jurisdictions that banned life without parole for juveniles."¹³² Here, the number itself—twenty-eight—is not dispositive. Given that the Court proceeded to evaluate other factors in *Graham* (which only had a count of thirteen), and detected a national consensus in *Atkins*, *Simmons*, and *Graham*, the fact that more than half of the jurisdictions in the country do not permit life

---

(indicating that twenty-two states and the federal government authorize the punishment).
130 Kennedy v. Louisiana, 554 U.S. 407, 423 (2008).
131 *Simmons*, 543 U.S. at 564 ("When *Atkins* was decided, [thirty] States prohibited the death penalty for the mentally retarded . . . . By a similar calculation in this case, [thirty] States prohibit the juvenile death penalty . . ..").
132 Smith, Sarma & Cull, at 2407–08.

without parole sentences for nonviolent offenses makes clear that a meaningful analysis of other consensus factors is warranted.[133]

---

[133] The other factors should be evaluated for an additional reason. Some legislatures that made it possible to punish individuals convicted of nonviolent offenses through life without parole sentences may not have been targeting the particular offenders who have actually been punished accordingly. Instead, law enforcement officials have enforced textually overbroad laws to punish individuals that legislators may have never envisioned. *See, e.g.*, Mandatory Minimum Penalties 2011, and accompanying text (describing legislation that Congress passed without its usual deliberation in order to rapidly respond to a high-profile criminal act, thereby overlooking the full impact of the legislation). This concept touches on a strand of the Eighth Amendment consensus jurisprudence that has arisen in previous cases at the Supreme Court. The Court has reasoned that it cannot divine legislators' intentions where the statutory scheme that renders a person eligible for the challenged punishment does so by circuitous or indirect means. *See, e.g.*, Graham v. Florida, 560 U.S. 48, 66–67 (2010) ("The Court confronted a similar situation in *Thompson*, where a plurality concluded that the death penalty for offenders younger than [sixteen] was unconstitutional. A number of States then allowed the juvenile death penalty if one considered the statutory scheme. As is the case here, those States authorized the transfer of some juvenile offenders to adult court; and at that point there was no statutory differentiation between adults and juveniles with respect to authorized penalties. The plurality concluded that the transfer laws show 'that the States consider [fifteen]-year-olds to be old enough to be tried in criminal court for serious crimes (or too old to be dealt with effectively in juvenile court), *but tells us nothing about the judgment these States have made regarding the appropriate punishment for such youthful offenders.*' . . . The same reasoning obtains here. Many States have chosen to move away from juvenile court systems and to allow juveniles to be transferred to, or charged directly in, adult court under certain circumstances. Once in adult court, a juvenile offender may receive the same sentence as would be given to an adult offender, including a life without parole sentence. But the fact that transfer and direct charging laws make life without parole possible for some juvenile nonhomicide

offenders does not justify a judgment that many States intended to subject such offenders to life without parole sentences . . .. [T]he many States that allow life without parole for juvenile nonhomicide offenders but do not impose the punishment should not be treated as if they have expressed the view that the sentence is appropriate.") (citations omitted); Miller v. Alabama, 132 S. Ct. 2455, 2472 (2012) ("We reasoned that in those circumstances, it was impossible to say whether a legislature had endorsed a given penalty . . .."). As one commentator has explained, "*Graham* and *Miller* also indicate that inadvertence in authorizing a challenged sentence may diminish the deference that would normally be shown to legislative policy choices." O'Hear, at 1126.

THE DIRECTION OF LEGISLATIVE CHANGE

The Court looks beyond the number of jurisdictions that authorize or prohibit a punishment and assesses the direction in which jurisdictions are moving. In *Atkins*, the Court held that "[i]t is not so much the number of these States [that prohibit the sentencing practice] that is significant, but the consistency of the direction of change."[134] In making the assessment about the direction of change, the Court evaluates whether jurisdictions have prohibited the challenged sentencing practice and whether others have reinstated or entrenched it.[135] "The Court's analysis thus

---

134 Atkins v. Virginia, 536 U.S. 304, 315 (2002).

135 *See* Smith, Sarma & Cull, , at 2410 ("In *Atkins*, the Court noted that a 'large number of States'—sixteen—took the death penalty off the table for mentally retarded offenders after the Court rejected the Eighth Amendment claim in *Penry v. Lynaugh*, and there was a 'complete absence of States passing legislation reinstating' the penalty for the same class of individuals. The Court also relied on 'direction' in *Simmons*, holding that 'the same consistency of direction of change' had 'been demonstrated' where no state reinstated the juvenile death penalty after *Stanford [v. Kentucky]* and five states prohibited it in fifteen years.") (footnotes omitted).

searches for uniformity in the direction, along with some (undefined) number of jurisdictions to undergird that shift."

There is widespread evidence that many jurisdictions have recently adopted laws that cut back on harsh mandatory minimum sentencing laws and habitual offender laws that historically have rendered nonviolent offenders eligible for life without parole sentences. Aside from California, however, it seems that no jurisdiction has passed a discrete law that specifically addresses the narrow sentencing practice at issue here. This does not mean that other jurisdictions have not also amended certain statutes to take life without parole off the table for nonviolent offenses; rather, it speaks to the difficulty of tracking such changes over time when statutes may provide for these sentences in a variety of ways. For example, a life without parole sentence may be imposed through mandatory minimums on the front-end or created through the abolition of parole on the back-end. Unlike other sentencing practices considered by the Court under the Eighth Amendment—which have generally been confined to a jurisdiction's murder statutes—the difficulty of identifying nonviolent life without parole-eligible offenses renders traditional "head counting" of states much more difficult. For this reason, an examination of actual usage of the punishment—how often the sentence is imposed— provides a more readily available and reliable gauge.

Political and legislative movement away from the types of laws that resulted in the lifetime incarceration of nonviolent offenders may still play a critical role in the consensus analysis. The evidence of such a movement was set out in includes the President's recent grants of clemency, state legislative reforms, and public statements from leading officials. There appear to be three possible avenues for this evidence to influence the Court. First, the Court could consider it relevant to the direction of legislative change factor even if the evidence is not totally on-point because it is not tailored to provide relief to individuals convicted of nonviolent offenses.[136] Second, the Court could consider this evidence relevant not to the legislative

---

[136] This might seem incongruous given that the Court has not attributed full-blown intent to legislatures that have made individuals eligible for certain punishments through complicated statutory schemes. *See supra* note 205. Although it might be odd for the Court to find that laws one or two steps removed from the question cannot be relied upon in one circumstance but can in the other, "[t]he Court's recent history demonstrates a steady extension in the Eighth Amendment's reach." Ian P. Farrell, *Abandoning Objective Indicia*, 122 Yale L.J. Online 303, 309 (2013). In fact, the Court has previously considered it persuasive that jurisdictions have passed laws making the punishment available but not for the type of offenses that define the constitutional challenge. *See* Enmund v. Florida, 458 U.S. 782, 792 (1982) ("Moreover, of the eight States which have enacted new death penalty statutes since 1978, none authorize capital punishment in such circumstances."). If certain jurisdictions have made life without parole available for some crimes but not nonviolent offenses that may be a development the Court considers. According to the ACLU, "LWOP is now used in [forty-nine] states," but individuals convicted of nonviolent offenses have received such sentences in only nine states. Turner & Bunting, at 20–23.

trend factor but instead to its independent judgment.[137] And, third, the Court could draw upon evidence related to these changes that fits more neatly into one of its doctrinal factors. For example, states that have recently passed laws prohibiting mandatory life without parole sentences for drug crimes will sentence fewer nonviolent offenders to the punishment moving forward. This means that the evidence of the broader movement has specific effects that the consensus analysis can detect through its determination of the number of sentences actually imposed.

---

[137] The independent judgment prong of the evolving standards of decency test is capacious and enables the Court to even consider evidence about the state of international law. See Roger P. Alford, Roper v. Simmons and Our Constitution in International Equipoise, 53 UCLA L. Rev. 1, 26 (2005) ("[T]he Court in Roper is suggesting that international equipoise may be invoked to confirm the Court's independent judgment of what the Constitution requires."). Under this prong, the Court could certainly give some, even if little, weight to the state-level legislative developments on habitual offender and mandatory minimum sentencing laws. 212. Smith, Sarma & Cull, at 2411.

THE NUMBER OF SENTENCES IMPOSED

The Supreme Court's consensus analysis does not end with the simple categorizing and tallying of jurisdictions' statutes; the Court also evaluates a "challenged penalty's usage when it decides the national consensus question."[138] Actual sentencing practices have long mattered in this context,[139] and recent cases demonstrate that a jurisdiction's usage of a legislatively authorized punishment can matter as much, if not more, than the fact that a statute permits it. In 2010:

> Sentencing practices . . . played an important—perhaps decisive—role in the Court's decision in *Graham* to bar life without the possibility of parole sentences for juveniles who commit nonhomicide offenses. More than three-dozen jurisdictions legislatively authorized life

---

138 *See id.* at 2411–13 (explaining how the Court considers the penalty's actual usage to determine whether there is a national consensus against a punishment).

139 *Id.* at 2412–13 (footnotes omitted); *see also* Sarma, at 199 (noting that the Court's 2014 decision in *Hall* "deepens the Court's commitment to analyzing usage indicators to determine if a state's legislative authorization of a punishment is a meaningful reflection of that state's popular will").

without parole . . . for juveniles who commit nonhomicide offenses. Florida argued that this widespread display of legislative support for the punishment foreclosed a finding that a consensus against the punishment exists. The Court labeled Florida's argument "incomplete and unavailing" and reiterated that "actual sentencing practices are an important part of the Court's inquiry into consensus." Where only 129 juvenile offenders were under a sentence of LWOP, the Court indicated there was "a consensus against its use."[140]

In situations in which a statute authorizes a particular challenged sentencing practice but the jurisdiction never or rarely utilizes it, the Court can look past the legislation itself to find that the lack of usage better reflects evolving standards of decency.

In earlier cases, the Court's usage analysis in consensus cases sometimes revealed that the challenged sentencing practice had been applied to literally a handful of individuals nationwide.[141] *Graham*

---

140 *See, e.g., Enmund*, 458 U.S. at 796 (finding relevant that "only three persons in that category [where the defendant did not commit the homicide, was not present when the killing took place, and did not participate in a plot or scheme to murder] are presently sentenced to die"); Kennedy v. Louisiana, 554 U.S. 407, 434 (2008) (finding it relevant that there were "only two individuals now on death row in the United States for a nonhomicide offense").

141 Graham v. Florida, 560 U.S. 48, 49 (2010).

clarified that the number of sentences handed down should be compared to the baseline number of defendants potentially eligible for the challenged sentence. "While more common in terms of absolute numbers than the sentencing practices in [other Eighth Amendment cases like *Enmund* and *Atkins*], the type of sentence at issue is actually as rare as those other sentencing practices when viewed in proportion to the opportunities for its imposition."[142] The Court thus determined that the 123 juvenile offenders sentenced to life without parole for nonhomicide crimes received a punishment "as rare" as the handful of death sentences highlighted in previous cases because in the year 2007 alone juveniles were arrested for over 380,000 aggravated assaults, forcible rapes, robberies, burglaries, drug offenses and arson. "Such infrequency in the imposition of a challenged sentence makes clear that overturning the sentence will

---

142 *See id.* at 65 (calculating the total number of arrests for aggravated assault, rape, robbery, burglary, drug offenses, and arson in 2007); *see also* Miller v. Alabama, 132 S. Ct. 2455, 2478–79 (2012) (Roberts, C.J., dissenting) ("The Court notes that *Graham* found a punishment authorized in [thirty-nine] jurisdictions unconstitutional, whereas the punishment it bans today is mandated in [ten] fewer. But *Graham* went to considerable lengths to show that although theoretical allowed in many States, the sentence at issue in that case was 'exceedingly rare' in practice. The Court explained that only 123 prisoners in the entire Nation were serving life without parole for nonhomicide crimes committed as juveniles, with more than half in a single State. It contrasted that with statistics showing nearly 400,000 juveniles were arrested for serious nonhomicide offenses in a single year. Based on the sentence's rarity despite the many opportunities to impose it, *Graham* concluded that there was a national consensus against life without parole for juvenile nonhomicide crimes.") (citations omitted).

not impose major disruptions on the day to-day functioning of state criminal justice systems . . . ."[143]

Two numbers seem to matter most in the analysis of sentencing practices: (1) the number of people who are sentenced to the challenged punishment; and (2) the number of people who are eligible to be sentenced to the challenged punishment. The first number may be thought of as the "numerator" and second number the "denominator" because dividing the first number by the second reveals (an estimate of) the percentage of individuals eligible for a punishment that actually receive it. The numbers generate for the Court a rough idea of how "unusual" a punishment is in reality.

Here, the relevant numerator appears to be in the ballpark of 3,300 to 4,500 prisoners. According to the ACLU "as of 2012, there were 3,278 prisoners serving life without parole for nonviolent drug and property crimes in the federal system and in nine states that provided such statistics . . . ."[144] That number may be somewhat higher because, as the ACLU acknowledges, "there may well be more such prisoners in [three] other states" that permit the challenged

---

143 Turner & Bunting, at 2; *id.* at 20 ("According to data collected and analyzed by the ACLU, 3,278 prisoners are serving LWOP for drug, property, and other nonviolent crimes in the United States as of 2012.").

144 *Id.* at 2; *see id.* at 24 (noting that Delaware, Virginia, and Nevada did not give ACLU data but have life without parole for nonviolent offenses, so "the total number of nonviolent LWOP prisoners nationwide is likely higher than the ACLU's data suggests").

punishment but did not disclose information. If one assumes for the sake of argument that the three jurisdictions that did not share information each had an average of 328 inmates under the sentence—the average determined by the 3,278 prisoners across the ten reporting jurisdictions—there would be an additional 984 relevant sentences. That estimate, likely a significant overestimate (given that the 3,278 figure includes the federal government's count of more than 2,000 offenders), would put the total number at 4,262. For the analysis here—a highly conservative one—we shall assume there are 4,500 prisoners serving life without parole for nonviolent offenses.

Initially, the total number of sentences at issue seems dramatically higher than in the other Eighth Amendment categorical ban cases. It is far beyond the two offenders in *Kennedy*, three offenders in *Enmund*, and even the 123 in *Graham*.[145] But, to be understood, the number must be contextualized; the numerator requires a denominator to obtain real meaning under this analysis. Indeed, it is when one tries to determine the denominator that the initial image gets shattered. The almost astronomical size of the denominator

---

145 *Crime in the United States 2013: Property Crime*, Fed. Bureau of Investigation (2013) https://www.fbi.gov/about-us/cjis/ucr/crime-inthe-u.s/2013/crime-in-the-u.s.-13/property-crime/property-crime-topic-page/propertycrimemainfinal [https://perma.cc/RDE6-X742].

demonstrates that life without parole sentences for nonviolent offenses ranks among the rarest sentences the Court has seen.

It is impossible to drum up an accurate guess for the number of nonviolent offenses (as defined earlier in this Article) that occur in any given year. In *Graham*, the Court faced a similar challenge of giving "attention ... to the base number of certain types of offenses" and it utilized the statistics that were readily available.[146] As a starting place, the Uniform Crime Reports (UCR) compiled by the Federal Bureau of Investigation (FBI) provide a yearly breakdown of property crimes. According to the FBI, property crime statistics "include[] the offenses of burglary, larceny-theft, [and] motor vehicle theft . . . ."[147] In 2013, "there were an estimated 8,632,512 property crime offenses in the nation."[148] This total provides a very

---

146 *Crime in the United States 2013: Persons Arrested*, Fed. Bureau of Investigation (2013) https://www.fbi.gov/about-us/cjis/ucr/crime-inthe-u.s/2013/crime-in-the-u.s.-2013/persons-arrested/persons-arrested [https://perma.cc/T9PD-D4ZD].

147 The fact that jurisdictions have been handing down the challenged punishment over the span of the past few decades is highly relevant. *See Graham*, 560 U.S. at 65 ("The numbers cited above reflect all current convicts in a jurisdiction's penal system, regardless of when they were convicted. It becomes all the clearer how rare these sentences are, even within the jurisdictions that do sometimes impose them, when one considers that a juvenile sentenced to life without parole is likely to live in prison for decades. Thus, these statistics likely reflect nearly all juvenile nonhomicide offenders who have received a life without parole sentence stretching back many years.").

148 In *Furman v. Georgia*, a plurality expressed concern that the death penalty was so infrequently applied that it was cruel and unusual where it estimated that only fifteen to twenty percent of

conservative estimate because it does not include any drug possession or distribution offenses. The UCR separately provides information about the number of arrests in a given year for particular categories of crime. This number includes information about arrests for drug abuse violations; in 2013, there were an estimated 1,501,043 arrests for this category of crimes.[149] Creating the most conservative estimate, we can assume a one hundred percent arrest rate for drug abuse violations and that arrests occurred one-to one for each drug crime. In other words, assume there were 1,501,043 drug crimes. Combined with the 8,632,512 property crimes, that would create a total estimate of 10,133,555 crimes for 2013 alone.

Even though it is extraordinarily difficult if not impossible to determine how many of these more than 10 million crimes would

---

eligible offenders received the punishment. 408 U.S. 238, 386 n.11 (1972) (Burger, C.J., dissenting) ("Although accurate figures are difficult to obtain, it is thought that from [fifteen percent] to [twenty percent] of those convicted of murder are sentenced to death in States where it is authorized."); see also Steven F. Shatz & Nina Rivkind, *The California Death Penalty Scheme: Requiem for Furman?*, 72 N.Y.U. L. Rev. 1283, 1288 (1997) ("[T]he Justices' conclusion that the death penalty was imposed only infrequently derived from their understanding that only [fifteen to twenty percent] of convicted murderers who were death-eligible were being sentenced to death"). That sentencing rate is roughly 337 to 450 times greater than the 0.0444% rate for nonviolent life without parole offenders generated above.

149 Smith, Sarma & Cull, at 2414 ("Although the Court has not explicitly considered geographic isolation as an independent variable in the national consensus analysis (as apart from the number of states that authorize a punishment), the Eighth Amendment cases indicate that it plays a role.").

have made a nonviolent offender eligible for a life sentence, the number is still instructive. Dealing with a similar dilemma in *Graham*, the Court found that:

> Although it is not certain how many of these numerous [~400,000] juvenile offenders were eligible for life without parole sentences, the comparison suggests that in proportion to the opportunities for its imposition, life without parole sentences for juveniles convicted of nonhomicide crimes is as rare as other sentencing practices found to be cruel and unusual.[150]

Here, too, the "comparison suggests" that life without parole sentences for nonviolent offenses are as rare as those juvenile life without parole punishments for nonhomicide crimes the Court held unconstitutional. Dividing the numerator by the denominator in *Graham* (123/380,480) yields a 0.0323% sentencing rate. Here, that same calculation (4,500/10,133,555) yields a 0.0444% sentencing rate. Both numbers represent very rough estimates; both numbers are infinitesimal; and both numbers reflect the sort of profoundly infrequent use that troubles the Court. Therefore, this factor—the number of sentences imposed—should weigh strongly in favor of an Eighth Amendment ban on the punishment.

---

150 *Graham*, 560 U.S. at 64 (relying on the fact that 77 of the 123 sentences had been handed down in Florida).

THE DEGREE OF GEOGRAPHIC ISOLATION

A factor the Court implicitly considers when dealing with a categorical challenge is the degree of the challenged punishment's geographic isolation. "Geographic isolation describes when a relatively small number of jurisdictions that authorize a punishment become responsible for the vast majority of the contested sentences imposed." This factor played a major role in *Graham* where the Court found that one jurisdiction had sentenced "[a] significant majority" of the individuals serving the challenged punishment. All of the remaining sentences had come from "just 10 states."[151]

The geographic distribution of sentences in *Graham* was particularly important because thirty-nine jurisdictions (thirty-seven states plus the District of Columbia and the federal system) statutorily permitted the challenged punishment.[152] However, the

---

151 Turner & Bunting, at 23; see also id. at 39 (showing the nine states are Alabama, Florida, Georgia, Illinois, Louisiana, Mississippi, Missouri, Oklahoma, and South Carolina).

152 See Turner & Bunting, supra note 4, at 16 (explaining that this number may actually be eleven, twelve, thirteen, or fourteen

Court found significant the "[a]ctual sentencing practices," which revealed that "only 11 jurisdictions nationwide in fact impose life without parole sentences on juvenile nonhomicide offenders—and most of those do so quite rarely—while 26 States, the District of Columbia, and the Federal Government do not impose them despite apparent statutory authorization." Geographic isolation and infrequent usage combined in *Graham* to undermine the states' claim that there was no consensus against a punishment because of the sheer number of jurisdictions that technically permitted it.

Life without parole sentences for nonviolent offenders share a similar distributive pattern to the sentences struck down in *Graham*. To start, the number of jurisdictions that actually utilize the sentence is much lower than the number that technically authorize it. "In nine of these [twenty-two] states [and in the federal system], prisoners are currently serving life-without-parole sentences for a nonviolent offense . . .." That number decreased by one in 2015 because Missouri removed the lone prisoner under such a sentence.[153] In other words, fourteen of the twenty-three authorizing jurisdictions do not actually use the punishment. Moreover, where Florida was responsible for a majority of sentences at issue in *Graham*, "[n]early two-thirds of these prisoners [sentenced to life without parole for

---

because three states did not respond to the ACLU's records requests).

153 *See also* Graham v. Florida, 560 U.S. 48, 65 (2010) (noting that these numbers need to be put in the context of the span of many years in which individuals could be receiving these lives without parole sentences).

nonviolent offenses]— sixty-three percent—are in the federal system."[238] Only eight other jurisdictions use the challenged punishment.

SUMMARY OF THE NATIONAL CONSENSUS ANALYSIS

The case that there is now a national consensus against life without parole sentences for nonviolent offenses appears even stronger than the consensus evidence that prevailed in *Graham*. Substantially more jurisdictions—fifteen additional states—prohibit the challenged punishment. While the total number of individuals eligible for relief is far greater here, the proportion of individuals under the sentence compared to the relevant baseline crime statistics strongly suggests that both sentences are exceedingly rare.[240] Finally, the evidence of geographic isolation here is nearly identical to the evidence in *Graham*: less than half of the jurisdictions that permit the punishment actually deploy it, and one jurisdiction in particular generates a significant percentage of the sentences. Against this backdrop, it appears that there is more than enough evidence to support a judicial finding that there is a national consensus against life without parole sentences for nonviolent offenses.

EVALUATING THE SUPREME COURT'S INDEPENDENT JUDGMENT

In exercising its independent judgment, the Supreme Court considers "the culpability of the offenders at issue in light of their crimes and characteristics, along with the severity of the punishment in question . . . . In this inquiry the Court also considers whether the challenged sentencing practice serves legitimate penological goals."[154]

---

[154] *See, e.g.*, Roper v. Simmons, 543 U.S. 551, 569 (2005) (noting that juveniles have a "lack of maturity and an underdeveloped sense of responsibility" (quoting Johnson v. Texas, 509 U.S. 350, 367 (1993))); *id.* (noting that "juveniles are more vulnerable or susceptible to negative influences and outside pressures"); *id.* at 570 (noting that "the character of a juvenile is not as well formed as that of an adult").

THE CULPABILITY OF THE OFFENDERS IN LIGHT OF THEIR CRIMES

Culpability matters. In evaluating categorical challenges, the Court's culpability analysis turns on whether the challenge is based on "characteristics of the offender" or "the nature of the offense."[155] In challenges based on characteristics that define a specific class of offenders, the Court has not sought to determine a specific offender's level of culpability; instead, it has drawn conclusions about culpability based on characteristics that generally apply to members within the class. In *Simmons* and *Graham*, that class of offenders was juvenile offenders; in *Atkins* and *Hall*, the class consisted of offenders with intellectual disabilities. With respect to both classes, the Court found substantial reasons to treat their culpability as relatively limited, particularly when compared to fully functioning adult offenders.

---

155 *See, e.g.*, Atkins v. Virginia, 536 U.S. 304, 318 (2002) (noting that offenders with intellectual disabilities "have diminished capacities to understand and process information, to communicate, to abstract from mistakes and learn from experience, to engage in logical reasoning, to control impulses, and to understand the reactions of others").

For challenges based on the nature of the offense, the Court assesses the severity of the crime in light of the sentence. In *Coker*, the Court explained that the serious crime of rape deserves a weighty punishment but not a punishment that was only otherwise available for the undoubtedly graver crime of murder. According to the Court:

> Rape is without doubt deserving of serious punishment; but in terms of moral depravity and of the injury to the person and to the public, it does not compare with murder, which does involve the unjustified taking of human life. . . . . We have the abiding conviction that the death penalty, which 'is unique in its severity and irrevocability,' . . . is an excessive penalty for the rapist who, as such, does not take human life.[156]

The Court revisited the point in *Kennedy*, stating that with respect to capital punishment "there is a distinction between intentional first- degree murder on the one hand and nonhomicide crimes against individual persons . . . on the other."[157]

To date, the Court has not considered a categorical challenge based on the nonviolent nature of the offenses. There is no doubt that these offenses stand in stark contrast to the murders, rapes, and robberies

---

156 Coker v. Georgia, 433 U.S. 584, 598 (1977) (plurality opinion) (quoting Gregg v. Georgia, 428 U.S. 153, 187 (1976)).
157 Kennedy v. Louisiana, 554 U.S. 407, 438 (2008).

contemplated in the earlier landmark Eighth Amendment cases. Nonviolent crimes are not even crimes against individual persons as the Court described in *Kennedy* because by definition the offenses involve no harm or threat of harm to people. In an important way, these offenses are thus two full steps removed from the homicide crimes that in some circumstances warrant capital punishment and one step removed from the violent nonhomicide crimes for which the Court has found the death penalty unconstitutional. It follows that the Court would and should recognize (and perhaps even constitutionalize) the distinction between crimes against persons and nonviolent offenses.[158]

---

[158] According to at least one commentator, the Court has already relied on the distinction several times in the gross disproportionality context. *See* Kevin White, Comment, *Construing the Outer Limits of Sentencing Authority: A Proposed Bright-Line Rule for Noncapital Proportionality Review*, 2011 B.Y.U. L. Rev. 567, 587 (2011) ("[T]he fundamental distinction of whether an offense is nonviolent or violent has constituted a significant factor, if not the most significant factor, in the Court's assessment of the gravity of crimes.").

THE SEVERITY OF THE PUNISHMENT IN QUESTION

Another consideration relevant to the independent judgment analysis is the severity of the punishment. The precedent indicates that the Court's evaluative posture can be described in the following way: the more serious the punishment, the more serious the scrutiny. On several occasions, "[t]he Court has recognized the severity of sentences that deny convicts the possibility of parole."[159] In *Graham*, the Court described how life without parole sentences share important similarities to death sentences: "The State does not execute the offender sentenced to life without parole, but the sentence alters the offender's life by a forfeiture that is irrevocable. It deprives the convict of the most basic liberties without giving hope of restoration . . .." The Eighth Amendment cases suggest that the Court will apply substantial independent scrutiny to the life without parole sentences at issue. In short, the Court recognizes that this punishment is "the second most severe penalty permitted by law" and the most severe punishment available for nearly all crimes but murder.[160]

---

[159] Graham v. Florida, 560 U.S. 48, 70 (2010).
[160] Harmelin v. Michigan, 501 U.S. 957, 1001 (1991) (Kennedy, J., concurring in part and concurring in judgment).

THE VALIDITY OR INVALIDITY OF PENOLOGICAL GOALS

The Court's independent judgment analysis evaluates whether a challenged punishment serves any legitimate penological goals. Four traditional goals and justifications for punishment have garnered the Court's recognition: deterrence, retribution, rehabilitation, and incapacitation.[252] This Part considers each in turn.

DETERRENCE

Deterrence is a justification for punishment premised on the theory that the punishment can deter individuals from breaking the law. Two aspects in particular may contribute to a punishment's potential effectiveness as a deterrent – the certainty that the punishment will apply and the severity of the punishment.

The severity of a life without parole sentence is nearly without match. One might be tempted to believe that this maximally harsh sentence would thus clearly yield the greatest deterrent value when compared to other punishments. However, "there is little evidence that increases in the length of already long prison sentences yield general deterrent effects that are sufficiently large to justify their social and economic costs."[161] Indeed, the general proposition that sentence severity effectively deters crime is being called into question. Years of research and results from study after study have led many criminologists to conclude "[t]here is no plausible body of

---

[161] Ewing v. California, 538 U.S. 11, 25 (2003).

evidence that supports policies based on this premise [that harsh sentences deter] . . . ."[162]

Compared to punishment severity, the certainty of punishment is much more likely to provide a deterrent effect.[163] According to a leading expert on deterrence, "evidence in support of the deterrent effect of various measures of the certainty of punishment is far more convincing and consistent than for the severity of punishment."[164] Yet, the type of certainty that generally accepted research has demonstrated can have a deterrent effect is an offender's certainty that he will be apprehended. This type of certainty should be distinguished from the certainty that a particular sentence will be given. "Consequently, the conclusion that certainty, not severity, is the more effective deterrent is more precisely stated as *certainty of apprehension* and not the severity of the legal consequence ensuing from apprehension is the more effective deterrent." In other words, harsh sentencing regimes like life without parole have not been proven to have deterrent effects along the certainty dimension.

---

[162] Daniel S. Nagin, *Deterrence in the Twenty-First Century*, 42 Crime & Just. 199, 201 (2013).

[163] Anthony N. Doob & Cheryl Marie Webster, *Sentence Severity and Crime: Accepting the Null Hypothesis*, 30 Crime & Just. 143, 146 (2003).

[164] Raymond Paternoster, *How Much Do We Really Know About Criminal Deterrence?*, 100 J. Crim. L. & Criminology 765, 818 (2010) ("[T]here does seem to be a modest inverse relationship between the perceived certainty of punishment and crime, but no real evidence of a deterrent effect for severity . . . .").

With respect to life without parole sentences for nonviolent crimes, there are reasons to believe that certainty does not play a meaningful role in deterring offenders. To the extent perceptions reflect reality in the deterrence realm, a potential nonviolent offender is likely to be less concerned about apprehension than the potential violent offender because arrest rates for nonviolent crimes are much lower. More importantly, there is no basis to believe that potential offenders would envision receiving a life without parole sentence for nonviolent offenses because even among those individuals apprehended, very few actually end with this punishment. The sentence's rarity—it's imposition in some microscopic percentage of nonviolent cases—undermines its ability to deter.[165]

On the whole, deterrence may provide some support for the challenged sentencing practice, but that support is underwhelming. Standing alone, it seems that the deterrence rationale for sentencing nonviolent offenders to life without parole sentences "does not overcome other objections . . . ."[166] Therefore, the Court must decide what it makes of the other penological justifications as well.

---

165 Graham v. Florida, 560 U.S. 48, 72 (2010) (noting that individuals are less likely to take the punishment into consideration when making decisions to offend "particularly . . . when that punishment is rarely imposed").
166 Kennedy v. Louisiana, 554 U.S. 407, 441 (2008).

RETRIBUTION

Retribution describes the theory that punishment can be valid if the state uses it to ensure that an individual who commits a wrong gives up something—for example, freedom—in return. On this theory, the offender deserves to be punished because he has harmed a victim or society. The Court has described the "goal of retribution" as fulfilling "society's and the victim's interests in seeing that the offender is repaid for the hurt he caused."[167]

Imposing life without parole sentences on individuals who have committed nonviolent offenses takes retribution beyond its breaking point. Retribution relies on the idea that an "offender receive exactly the amount of punishment he deserves for the crime committed, and receive no more or no less."[168] It is difficult to imagine that our society countenances the notion that someone should be locked up forever without the possibility of release because she committed a

---

[167] Andrew D. Leipold, *Recidivism, Incapacitation, and Criminal Sentencing Policy*, 3 U. St. Thomas L.J. 536, 541 (2006) ("[O]ne simple explanation for the increasing prison population is that incapacitation works.").

[168] Ewing v. California, 538 U.S. 11, 26 (2003).

crime that did no direct harm to another person. Therefore, "there are certainly some crimes that, particularly . . . nonviolent crimes, may not be justifiable for Eighth Amendment purposes by the penological goal of retribution."[169] As the Court has put it, "retribution is a legitimate reason to punish, but it cannot support the sentence at issue here."

---

[169] *See, e.g.*, Jamie Fellner, *Graying Prisoners*, N.Y. Times (Aug. 18, 2013), http://www.nytimes.com/2013/08/19/opinion/graying-prisoners.html [http://perma.cc/FPP6-MF99] ("Recidivism studies consistently show declining rates of crime with age."); Leipold, *supra* note 270, at 555 ("An astonishing 82% of those inmates who are released at age 14-17 are likely to be re-arrested, while fewer than half (45%) of those age 45 and above will be.").

REHABILITATION

Rehabilitation refers to the penological goal of treating and training offenders so that they can effectively reintegrate into society and become law-abiding individuals. It is premised on the theory that some causes of criminal behavior can be addressed. As far as the life without parole punishment is concerned, rehabilitation is not and could not be a goal. "A sentence of life imprisonment without parole . . . cannot be justified by the goal of rehabilitation. The penalty forswears altogether the rehabilitative ideal. By denying the defendant the right to reenter the community, the State makes an irrevocable judgment about that person's value and place in society."[170] As one commentator put it: "Life without parole, by definition, is a judgment that an individual cannot be rehabilitated."

---

170 *Graham*, 560 U.S. at 71; *see also* Enmund v. Florida, 458 U.S. 782, 801 (1982) ("Putting Enmund to death to avenge two killings that he did not commit and had no intention of committing or causing does not measurably contribute to the retributive end of ensuring that the criminal gets his just deserts."). Indeed, it appears the Court has questioned retribution's validity or at least indicated that it is the least persuasive penological justification because it is the one "that most often can contradict the law's own ends." *Kennedy*, 554 U.S. at 420. "When the law punishes by death" and other extremely harsh punishments, "it risks its own sudden descent into brutality, transgressing the constitutional commitment to decency and restraint." *Id.*

INCAPACITATION

Incapacitation represents the concept that crimes can be prevented by physically removing offenders from society and thereby curtailing their opportunities to commit further crimes. It turns on the assumption that the incarcerated offender, if free, would engage in more criminal activity. Policymakers often rely upon incapacitation as the key tool for reducing recidivism.

The Supreme Court has recognized that incapacitation can be a powerful justification for some harsh sentencing regimes. In *Ewing*, the Court noted that "recidivism is a serious public safety concern . . . throughout the Nation." In terms of addressing that concern, "it is hard to dispute the efficacy of imprisonment: those in prison don't commit any new crimes except against guards and other inmates, and so by extending the periods of imprisonment . . . we extend the period where the inmate cannot re-offend." Though there are clear societal and public safety benefits to keeping individuals likely to engage in more criminal activity behind bars, there are also substantial costs and concerns – many of which are now being raised and discussed by lawmakers around the country.

When a court hands down a life without parole sentence, that sentence represents a "determination that the individual *will always* be dangerous to society." These determinations are often problematic because "incontrovertible scientific evidence demonstrates that future dangerousness determinations are, at best, wildly speculative." When sentences get it wrong, there is no recourse. At no point will any judicial or executive body be asked to revisit the initial assessment because there is no opportunity at all for parole. Life without parole sentences also prove insensitive to the reality that recidivism rates decline as offenders get older. For this reason, it is "quite doubtful . . . whether such a long and inflexible sentence as LWOP can ever be justified on incapacitation grounds, given the very low recidivism rates of elderly ex-convicts."

Particularly in the context of individuals convicted of nonviolent offenses, the financial costs of lifetime incarceration may outweigh the risks that come with less severe term-of-year sentences or even the mere possibility of paroling an inmate who has served some significant amount of time. "Keeping the elderly and infirm in prison is extraordinarily costly."[278] And, though there are costs on the other side (for example, the economic costs of additional crimes committed by released offenders), the marginal incapacitate benefit of denying individuals the opportunity to even seek parole seems slim.

As the Court recognized in *Ewing* and again in *Graham*, incapacitation is "an important goal." It is also a goal that is undoubtedly achieved when someone is sentenced to die in prison; that individual will never commit a crime outside of the prison walls again. But, achieving that goal comes at a great cost. It means denying outright the possibility of release to many individuals who would not commit another crime or who will be rehabilitated. And, it means reaffirming the idea that nonviolent crimes can warrant an extraordinarily harsh punishment just short of the death penalty. While incapacitation

INTERNATIONAL OPINION

In its independent judgment analysis, the Court sometimes considers how other countries approach the challenged punishment. This factor—the status of international opinion—is never "controlling" of the "outcome," but it "does provide respected" input for the Court's "own conclusions."[171] Where the Court has found a punishment unconstitutional under its Eighth Amendment categorical analysis, it "has treated the laws and practices of other nations and international agreements as relevant . . . because the judgment of the world's nations that a particular sentencing practice is inconsistent with basic principles of decency demonstrates that the Court's rationale has respected reasoning to support it."[172]

On the question of life without parole sentences, the international community appears to have largely rejected the punishment, especially for nonviolent offenses. According to the ACLU:

---

171 Roper v. Simmons, 543 U.S. 551, 578 (2005).
172 Turner & Bunting, at 11

Today, the United States is virtually alone in its willingness to sentence nonviolent offenders to die behind bars . . .. Such sentences are rare in other countries and were recently ruled a violation of human rights in a landmark decision by the European Court of Human Rights that would require an opportunity for review of the sentences of 49 prisoners serving LWOP (for murder) in the United Kingdom—one of only two countries in Europe that still sentence prisoners to LWOP.[173]

Moreover, the Rome Statute, which has been signed by almost 100 nations, requires that life sentences for all crimes, including the most violent ones, be subject to review after twenty-five years. There are no readily available figures detailing the number of individuals under sentence of life without parole for nonviolent offenses, but only about twenty percent of countries use life without parole at all, and of those a majority only imposes it for violent offenses in limited circumstances.[174]

---

[173] *See id.* (demonstrating that, by imposing life without parole sentences for crimes other than murder, the United States is virtually alone amongst Western democracies).

[174] *See, e.g.*, Turner & Bunting, at 200 (explaining that the United States is not among the 100 countries that have signed the Rome statute).

The international opinion factor does not clearly establish universal disapproval of the punishment, but it points toward a widespread rejection. The factor here plays a role similar to the one it played in *Graham*. There, the Court found that "only 11 nations authorize life without parole for juvenile offenders under any circumstances; and only 2 of them [including the United States] . . . ever impose the punishment in practice." So, even where the evidence of international consensus is not as powerful as it was in *Simmons*— where the U.S. was "the only country in the world that continue[d] to give official sanction" to the challenged practice—the factor can still confirm an independent judgment that life without parole is an excessive punishment for nonviolent offenses.

WHAT ACADEMIC 'S STATE

Consecutive Sentences as Defacto Life Sentences

Professor Connie de la Vega Writes[175] When offenders commit multiple offenses, some countries issue consecutive or cumulative sentences, which are served one after the other. Others issue concurrent sentences, which are all served simultaneously, entitling the inmate to release after he or she has served the term of the longest sentence, or in other words merge the punishments for lesser offenses into the most serious one. Some countries allow both types of sentencing. Whether conduct constitutes one or several crimes brings into question whether a conviction can be entered for all the applicable offenses as well as whether the total amount of punishment should be increased. [176] Courts and legislatures must then decide when criminal acts should be treated as one offense or several.

---

175 U.S. Sentencing Practices in a Global Context Professor Connie de la Vega ,Amanda Solter Soo-Ryun Kwon, Dana Marie Isaac May 2012

176 Carl-Friedrich Stuckenberg, *A Cure for Concursus Delictorum in International Criminal Law?* 16 Criminal Law Forum 361, 362 (2005).

The practice of multiplying charges and convictions for the same criminal act is potentially problematic for several reasons. It can result in duplicative penalties that lose sight of the fact that there has been only one transaction. In criminal law, these interests can be protected to some degree by good legislative draftsmanship, deletion of duplicative criminal provisions, and being watchful of "legislative proliferation." Consecutive sentences can become *de facto* life without parole sentences when the possibility of parole is moved beyond the expected lifetime of the defendant, such as when sentences stack up to be many decades long or a defendant is issued multiple life sentences. [177]

A systemic problem in the United States is that courts have not understood double counting, that is punishing one wrong as if it were two or more, as a major issue. As a result, neither courts nor legislatures have offered comprehensive remedies. For example, a defendant who makes a single sale of narcotics can be handed three consecutive terms for violating three laws: sale of narcotics outside the original stamped package, sale of narcotics not pursuant to the appropriate Treasury order forms, and sale of narcotics known by

---

[177] Daniel Engber, *Isn't One Life Sentence Enough*? Slate, Aug. 19, 2005, *available at*
http://www.slate.com/articles/news_and_politics/explainer/2005/08/ isnt_one_life_sentence_enough.html (last visited Apr. 12, 2012). For example, Dennis Rader, sentenced to 10 consecutive life sentences for the murder of 10 people, will be eligible for parole after having served a minimum of 175 years.

the seller to have been illegally imported.[178] In another example, if a defendant deposits a check obtained by fraud, he can be found guilty of both the National Stolen Property Act as well as the mail fraud statute.[179] A person who robs a bank can be consecutively sentenced for both entering a bank with intent to commit robbery and for robbery.[180] An accountant who doctors his account books to defraud the Internal Revenue Service can have his sentence enhanced twice: once for his use of a special skill and again for using sophisticated means to hide the crime.[181]

Defendants are commonly prosecuted for preparatory crimes, such as conspiracy to commit other crimes, as well as have their sentences enhanced for particular intent, such as under hate crime statutes.[182] The same wrong can be prosecuted as multiple offenses, resulting in decades- to centuries-long sentences for first-time non-violent offenders, sentences sometimes far surpassing those for murderers. There can be a tendency for such sentences serving symbolic functions in high-profile cases. *Daniel Enrique Guevara Vilca, 26, was sentenced to 154 years in prison in November 2011 for 454*

---

178 Gore v. United States, 357 U.S. 386 (1958).
179 Pereira v. United States, 347 U.S. 1 (1954). The federal statutes held to have been violated were 18 U.S.C. § 2314 (1952) and the mail fraud statute, 18 U.S.C.§ 1341.
180 Prince v. United States, 352 U.S. 322 (1957).
181 U.S. Sentencing Guidelines Manual, §§ 3B1.3 and 2T1.1(b)(2) (2010).
182 *See* Apprendi v. New Jersey, 120 S.Ct. 2348 (2010).

counts of possessing child pornography. Each count represented one image. This sentence was longer than some for manslaughter, aggravated assault, child molestation, and rape of minors.[183] Sholam Weiss was convicted of 78 counts, including racketeering, money laundering and fraud charges, for stealing money from National Heritage Life Insurance and received 845 years in prison.[184] His projected release date is in 2754.

Norman Schmidt, charged with conspiracy to commit mail fraud, wire fraud, and securities fraud, as well as actual mail fraud, wire fraud, and securities fraud, was sentenced to 330 years.[185] In California, Rodrigo Caballero was convicted of three counts of attempted murder for shooting at three teens and wounding one when he was 16.[186] He was sentenced to 110 years to life for three consecutive life terms. He will be eligible for parole in 2112, when

---

183 Jacob Carpenter, *East Naples Man's Life Sentence for Child Porn Too Harsh, Attorney Says*, Naples News, Nov. 3, 2011, http://www.naplesnews.com/news/2011/nov/03/east-naples-mans-life-sentence-child-porn-too-hars/.

184 William K. Rashbaum, *845 Years in Prison, If the Authorities Can Catch Him*, N. Y. Times, Mar. 9, 2000.

185 Press Release, U.S. Attorney's Office, District of Colorado, Norman Schmidt Sentenced to 330 Years in Federal Prison for Multi-Million Dollar "High Yield" Investment Fraud, *available at* http://www.justice.gov/usao/co/press_releases/archive/2008/April08/4_29_08.html (last accessed Feb. 23, 2012).

186 Bob Egelko, *Court: Teen's 110-year Sentence is Constitutional*, SFGate, Jan. 19, 2011, *available at* http://www.sfgate.com/cgi-bin/article.cgi?f=/c/a/2011/01/18/BA2R1HAT4J.DTL

he is 122 years old.[187] *He is therefore effectively sentenced to die in prison.*

U.S. state and federal courts have repeatedly rejected claims that consecutive sentences constitute cruel and unusual punishment.[188] Courts have permitted 20 years imprisonment (two consecutive 10-year sentences) for passing bad checks [189] and 30 years for wire fraud (six consecutive 5-year sentences), sentences which in other countries are reserved for violent crimes.[190]

Historically, in common law, judges were entrusted with the decision whether sentences for discrete offenses should be served consecutively or concurrently.[191] Under U.S. federal law, federal courts can issue concurrent and consecutive sentences. [192]Similarly,

---

[187] Brief for Appellant at 1, California v. Rodrigo Caballero, No. B217709 (2nd App. District Div. 4, 2011).

[188] *See generally*, Howard J. Halperin, *Length of Sentence as Violation of Constitutional Provisions Prohibiting Cruel and Unusual Punishment*, 33 A.L.R. 3d 335 (1970).

[189] Boerngen v. U.S., 326 F.2d 326 (5th Cir. 1964).

[190] Lindsey v. U.S., 332 F.2d 688 (9th Cir. 1964).

[191] Oregon v. Ice, 555 U.S. 160 (2009).

[192] Crim. Pro. Code, 18 U.S.C. §3584(a). The statute states, "If multiple terms of imprisonment are imposed on a defendant at the same time, or if a term of imprisonment is imposed on a defendant who is already subject to an undischarged term of imprisonment, the terms may run concurrently or consecutively, except that the terms may not run consecutively for an attempt and for another offense that was the sole objective of the attempt. Multiple terms of imprisonment imposed at the same time run concurrently unless the court orders or the statute mandates that the terms are to run consecutively.

many states have enacted statutes or rules of criminal procedure or courts have issued case decisions to allow consecutive sentencing.[193] Some states establish a presumption of consecutive sentences with concurrent sentences issued only when the court explicitly lists its reasons for issuing its sentences simultaneously.[194] Some state laws *require* consecutive sentencing for certain crimes, such as crimes committed by a prisoner or

---

[193] Erin E. Goffette, Note, *Sovereignty in Sentencing: Concurrent and Consecutive Sentencing of a Defendant Subject to Simultaneous State and Federal Jurisdiction*, 37 Val. U. L. Rev. 1035, 1050, FN 67 (2003); See Alexander Bunin, *Time and Again: Concurrent and Consecutive Sentences Among State and Federal Jurisdictions,* Champion 34, Mar. 21, 1997

[194] These include Delaware, D.C., Florida, Louisiana, Montana, Virginia, Washington, West Virginia, and Wyoming. *See, e.g.*, Del. Code Ann. tit. 11, § 3901(d) (West 2012) (ordering that no term of imprisonment for a state offense shall be run concurrently with any other state sentence); D.C. Code Ann. § 23-112 (West 1996); Fla. Stat. Ann. § 921.16(1) (West 2012); La. Code Crim. Proc. Ann. art. 883 (West 2012) (mandating a presumption of consecutive sentences under specific conditions); Mont. Code Ann. § 46- 18-401(1)(a), (4) (West 2001); Va. Code Ann. § 19.2-308 (Michie 2000); Wash. Rev. Code Ann. § 9.92.080(3) (West 2012); W. VA. CODE § 61-11-21 (West 2000); see also Robertson v. Superintendent of Wise Corr. Unit, 445 S.E.2d 116, 117 (Va. 1994); Keith v. Leverette, 254 S.E.2d 700, 703 (W. Va. 1979); Apodaca v. State, 891P.2d 83, 85 (Wyo. 1995). *See* Brief of the National Association of Criminal Defense Lawyers as Amicus Curiae in Support of Respondent, Oregon v. Ice, 555 U.S. 160 (2009) (No. 07-901), 2008 WL 3539502, for comprehensive coverage of states' consecutive sentencing statutes.

escapee, sex offenses, other offenses committed while in possession of a firearm, or multiple offenses of the same statute.[195]

There has been little principled consistency in the United States as to whether sentences should run concurrently or consecutively.[196] As a result, there is an array of tests to assess whether two crimes are the same or not. The wide discretion given to judges and the multitude of legal tests to distinguish whether an act comprises more than one crime indicate that the problem of multiple offenses is one that has invited diverse judicial approaches that sometimes allow consecutive sentences and sometimes do not[197].

- The "Blockburger test" from *Blockburger v. United States* says that offenses are different if each requires proof of some fact that the other does not.[198] This test merges lesser included offenses, like robbery, into their aggravated versions, such as armed robbery because a robbery

---

[195] Erin E. Goffette, Note, *Sovereignty in Sentencing: Concurrent and Consecutive Sentencing of a Defendant Subject to Simultaneous State and Federal Jurisdiction*, 37 Val. U. L. Rev. 1035, 1050, FN 71 (2003).

[196] *See* 24 C.J.S. Criminal Law § 2098.

[197] *See* Phillip E. Johnson, *Multiple Punishment and Consecutive Sentences: Reflections on the Neal Doctrine*, 59 Cal. L. Rev. 357 (1970).

[198] Blockburger v. U.S., 284 U.S. 299 (1932). Though the Blockburger test is often referenced with respect to double jeopardy, it is also used to distinguish whether the same act has constituted more than one crime, such as in the issuance of multiple sentences

conviction needs no further proof than that required for armed robbery. The U.S. Sentencing Commission's Sentencing Guidelines acknowledges this need to avoid redundant counts by sorting greater and lesser included crimes.[199]

- The "same act or transaction" test, advocated by U.S. Supreme Court Justice William Brennan in several dissenting opinions, treats two offenses as the same if they arise from the same course of conduct, no matter how many crimes a prosecutor could allege and no matter the definitional differences between them.[200] While the Supreme Court has not adopted this test, 17 states have in order to ban successive prosecutions.

- Several state courts use a "single intent" test; if they were animated by a single criminal purpose, offenses are the same.[201] This prevents cumulative punishment when the

---

199 U.S. Sentencing Guidelines Manual, § 3D1.2 n.3 (2010).

200 State v. Truitt, 454 U.S. 1047 (1981) (Brennan, J., concurring); Ashe v. Swenson, 397 U.S. 436, 453 (1970) (Brennan, J., concurring); Brooks v. Oklahoma, 456 U.S.999, 1000 (1982) (Brennan, J., dissenting); Snell v. United States, 450 U.S. 957, 958 (1982) (Brennan, J., dissenting); Werneth v. Idaho, 449 U.S. 1129, 1130 (1981)(Brennan, J., dissenting) (joined by Marshall, J.); Duncan v. Tennessee, 405 U.S. 127, 131 (1972) (Brennan, J., dissenting) (joined by Douglas, J., Marshall, J.).

201 George C. Thomas III, *The Prohibition of Successive Prosecutions for the Same Offense: In Search of a Prohibition*, 71 Iowa L. Rev. 323, 376 (1986) (describing range of "same offense" test).

same conduct violates multiple laws or is difficult to break into units for prosecution.

With the proliferation of laws at both state and federal levels in the United States, a broad range of conduct has become criminalized.[202] The explosion of federal law creating over 4,000 crimes means that federal prosecution is possible at the same time state prosecution is, which sometimes means that sentences must be served consecutively in first a federal prison and then a state prison, or vice versa[203] In 2010, the Supreme Court issued a unanimous decision that a federal gun statute263 tacking on an extra mandatory minimum of five years for gun possession, seven years for banishment, or 10 years for discharge for persons convicted of a drug or violent crime was permissible.[204] The decision confirmed that such sentences are not only mandatory minimums, but also consecutive, so that they must be imposed in addition to any other sentence, including the sentence for the underlying drug offense or

---

202 *Rough Justice in America, Too Many Law, Too Many Prisoners*, The Economist, Jul. 22, 2010, http://www.economist.com/node/16636027 (last accessed Apr. 9, 2012). Criminalized conduct includes "interstate transport of water hyacinths, trafficking in unlicensed dentures, or misappropriating the likeness of Woodsy Owl."

203 *See* Note, Erin E. Goffette, *Sovereignty in Sentencing: Concurrent and Consecutive Sentencing of a Defendant Subject to Simultaneous State and Federal Jurisdiction*, 37 Val. U. L. Rev. 1035 (2003); *Rough Justice in America, Too Many Law, Too Many Prisoners*, The Economist, Jul. 22, 2010.

204 Abbott v. Gould, 131 S. Ct. 18 (2010).

other crime of violence.[205] Prosecutors can effectively seek an additional five-year sentence for mere gun possession at the same time of the commission of a crime, even if the gun was not used in the commission of the crime.

The issuance of consecutive sentences, particularly when paired with mandatory minimums can result in *de facto* life imprisonment sentences. Consecutive sentences amounting to life or near-life sentences, particularly for non-violent offenses such as selling drugs prioritize retributive interests. Most importantly, such sentences neglect the possibility that offenders can be rehabilitated.

Weldon Angelo's, a then 24-year-old music producer in Utah with no prior convictions, was sentenced in federal court for three related marijuana sales of about $350 each. Since he possessed a weapon during the course of these sales, the sentencing judge was required to impose harsh consecutive penalties, regardless of the fact that the gun was never used in the sales. Angelos is currently

---

205 Abbott v. Gould, 131 S. Ct. 18 (2010); *U.S. Supreme Court Rules Against Abbott and Gould,* Families Against Mandatory Minimums, http://www.famm.
org/courts/FAMMLegalBriefs/USSupremeCourtrulesagainstAbbottandGould.aspx (last visited Apr. 13, 2012).

serving a 55-year sentence with no possibility of parole during that time in federal prison.[206]

Atiba Parker was convicted in Mississippi of two counts of sale of cocaine and one count of possession of cocaine when he was 29. He received a total of three sentences that run consecutively for a total of 42 years. His projected release date is 2048, when he will be 71.[207]

Though international human rights law is silent on consecutive sentencing sentences, the United States' obligations to orient its prisons system towards rehabilitation are violated by uncapped consecutive sentences, which become *de facto* life sentences. There is little international law on how multiple offenses tried at the same time (*concursus delictorum*) should be punished.[208] The guiding principle in international criminal law and case law established by the *ad hoc* tribunals, the International Criminal Tribunal for the Former Yugoslavia and the International Criminal Tribunal for Rwanda, is that the convict's final penalty should reflect the entire

---

206 *Weldon Angelos*, Families Against Mandatory Minimums, http://www.famm.org/facesofFAMM/FederalProfiles/WeldonAngelos.aspx (last visited Apr.

207 *Atiba Parker – Mississippi*, Families Against Mandatory Minimums, http://www.famm.org/ProfilesofInjustice/StateProfiles/AtibaParker.aspx (lastvisited April 8, 2012).

208 Silvia D'Ascoli, Sentencing in International Criminal Law 129 (2011).

range of criminal conduct and his or her overall culpability, the so-called "totality principle."[209] At the *ad hoc* courts, judges could decide on whether sentences would be issued consecutively or concurrently without specifying the sentence for each charge or count.

However, at the International Criminal Court, the judges must pronounce a separate sentence for each crime and then a joint sentence specifying the total period of imprisonment. The maximum sentence must be no less than the highest individual sentence pronounced and is capped at either 30 years or life imprisonment, which is itself reviewable after 25 years. Comparative Country Information on Consecutive Sentences Over three-quarters of the countries in the world regulate consecutive sentencing more stringently than the United States they issue sentences concurrently, they cap consecutive sentences at a number of years, or they merely enhance the sentence for the most serious offense. The U.S. is in a minority of countries (21%) that allow uncapped consecutive sentences for multiple crimes arising out of one act. The largest block of countries uses concurrent sentences, where the punishment for the most serious offense absorbs those for less serious offenses (46%). Many countries do allow consecutive sentences but cap them

---

209 *Id.*; Kunarac et al, TJ, 22 February 2001, para 551; Prosecutor v. Vasiljevic, Case No IT-98-32-T, Trial Judgment, Nov. 29, 2002, para 266; Delalic et al, AJ, Feb. 20, 2001, paras 429-430.

anywhere from 15 years to life (26%). A small group of countries issues one sentence for multiple offenses, but it is enhanced and capped (6%).

Many countries with common law traditions use both consecutive and concurrent sentences and give the judge discretion in imposing one or the other. In many civil law countries, the defendant may be tried and convicted of two or more distinct offenses growing out of a single course of conduct but may only be punished for the most severe.[210] Many of those countries have statutory language stating that if there is conjunction between several crimes, only one sentence of imprisonment is imposed, and it cannot exceed the maximum allowed by law to punish the most serious offense.[211] The legal concept is that the punishment meted out for the most severe offense is deemed sufficient or that lesser offenses are absorbed into the most serious offense. Some countries allow for a mere enhancement of the maximum for the most serious offense. Some countries' statutes provide for concurrent sentencing when one course of conduct violates several criminal provisions and for consecutive sentencing when several discrete acts violate several criminal provisions.

---

210 J. A. C. Grant, *The Lanza Rule of Successive Prosecutions*, 32 Colum. L. Rev. 1309, 1323 (1932).

211 Carl-Friedrich Stuckenberg, *A Cure for Concursus Delictorum in International Criminal Law?* 16 Criminal Law Forum 361, 371 (2005) (this is sometimes called "subsidiarity" or "consumption").

The problem of multiple sentences in the United States is under recognized, leading to lengthy consecutive sentences that are out of step with the seriousness of the crimes. Consecutive sentencing amounting to a time span exceeding a lifetime is in effect the equivalent of life without parole sentencing, depriving the offender of review for rehabilitation.

"A legislative mitigation of the penalty for a particular crime represents a legislative judgment that the lesser penalty or the different treatment is sufficient to meet the legitimate ends of the criminal law. Nothing is to be gained by imposing the more severe penalty after such a pronouncement [of lesser penalties]; the excess in punishment can, by hypothesis, serve no purpose other than to satisfy a desire for vengeance." The California Supreme Court in In re Estrada [212] Legislatures are tasked with delineating crimes and their corresponding penalties. As societies evolve, penal theories change. As a result, legislation may be passed which provides for a lesser punishment for a given crime than a previous legislature had mandated. Under international law, the decrease in penalty must apply retroactively to benefit the offender.[213] The principle behind this legal theory is that if a change in law results in a lesser penalty, an offender should not have to suffer a worse fate than an individual who by chance committed the same type of crime subsequent to the

---

212 In re Estrada, 63 Cal.2d 740, 745 (1965).
213 International Covenant on Civil and Political Rights, , art. 15.

change in law. Fairness dictates that an individual should receive the benefit of a legislature's progressive change of heart and be given the same punishment as someone who commits the same crime in a future moment in time.

Legal traditions have consistently prohibited the retroactive application of law that changes the legal status of an individual after the commission of a crime. This is known as *"[n]ullum crimen nulla poena sine praevia lege poenali:* no one is to be convicted or punished without a pre-existing criminal law in force."[214] The U.S. Constitution specifically prohibits these types of ex post facto laws in Article I, Section 9. Internationally, this prohibition is often combined with its logical corollary, which is the principle of retroactive application of beneficial or ameliorative law.[215] This principle is known as *lex mitior*, or the mercy doctrine, where laws are applied *in mitius* or "mildly." Retroactive amelioration requires that a law apply retroactively when it benefits the offender. If a change of law reduces a given penalty, it should apply to all offenders who have been affected by the law. This should potentially include those who have already received their punishment and are serving their sentence.

---

214 Scoppola v. Italy (No. 2), App. No. 10249/03, Eur. Ct. H.R. (2009).
215 Kenneth s. Gallant, The Principle of Legality in International and Comparative Criminal Law 273 (2009).

THE EVOLVING STANDARDS OF DECENCY AND RETROACTIVITY

CRUEL, UNUSUAL, AND COMPLETELY BACKWARDS: AN ARGUMENT FORRETROACTIVE APPLICATION OF THE EIGHTH AMENDMENT * Copyright © 2015 by Nishi Kumar. J.D., 2015, New York University School of Law; B.A., 2010, Columbia University. [216]

In 2012, the Supreme Court issued a landmark decision[217] substantially altering the long-held view that "death was different" under the Eighth Amendment, and thus required heightened procedural protections.[218] Prior to *Miller v. Alabama*, the Court had treated capital and noncapital sentencing differently,[219] holding that other severe punishments, particularly life-without-parole sentences given to minors, did not require the same protections. The 5–4 *Miller* majority crossed this divide, holding that defendants who were under eighteen at the time of their crimes were categorically less culpable than adult offenders, and were constitutionally entitled

---

216 CRUEL, UNUSUAL, AND COMPLETELY BACKWARDS: AN ARGUMENT FORRETROACTIVE APPLICATION OF THE EIGHTH AMENDMENT * Copyright © 2015 by Nishi Kumar. J.D., 2015, New York University School of Law; B.A., 2010, Columbia University.

217 Miller v. Alabama, 132 S. Ct. 2455 (2012).

218 *See* Gregg v. Georgia, 428 U.S. 153, 188 (1976) ("[T]he penalty of death is different in kind from any other punishment imposed under our system of criminal justice."); Woodson v. North Carolina, 428 U.S. 280, 303–04 (1976) ("[D]eath is a punishment different from all other sanctions in kind rather than degree.").

219 *See* Nancy J. King, *How Different Is Death? Jury Sentencing in Capital and Noncapital Cases Compared*, 2 OHIO ST. J. CRIM. L. 195, 214 (2004) (describing the discretion of juries in noncapital sentencing as compared to capital sentencing).

to individualized hearings before being sentenced to life without parole.[220] Furthermore, the majority emphasized that in the eyes of judges and juries, not only should death be different, but juveniles should be regarded differently as well.[221] Justice Kagan, writing for the majority, concluded that given the scientific information that had emerged regarding juveniles' brain development and capacity for rehabilitation, "appropriate occasions for sentencing juveniles to this harshest possible penalty will be uncommon" and reserved for those "whose crime reflects irreparable corruption."[222]

At the time of the decision, more than twenty-five hundred juvenile offenders were serving exactly the type of mandatory life-without parole sentences that the Court now deemed cruel and unusual, and thus beyond the power of Congress or the states to impose.[223]

---

220 *Miller*, 132 S. Ct. at 2469.

221 *Id.* at 2470; *see also* Elizabeth S. Scott, *"Children Are Different": Constitutional Values and Justice Policy*, 11 OHIO ST. J. CRIM. L. 71, 72 (2013) ("With increasing clarity, the Court has announced a broad principle grounded in developmental knowledge that 'children are different' from adult offenders and that these differences are important to the law's response to youthful criminal conduct." (quoting *Miller*, 132 S. Ct. at 2470)).

222 *Miller*, 132 S. Ct. at 2469.

223 Paul Elias, *Life Sentences for Juveniles: Should 2,500 Serving Life Without Parole Be Released?* HUFFINGTON POST (Aug. 19, 2012, 8:52 AM), http://www.huffingtonpost.com/ 2012/08/19/life-sentences-for-juveni_n_1806259.html; *see also* HUMAN RIGHTS WATCH,

WORLD REPORT 2009: EVENTS OF 2008, at 538, http://www.hrw.org/sites/default/files/ reports/wr2009_web.pdf (estimating that there are about 2502 juvenile offenders serving life-without-parole sentences in the United States).

Twenty-eight states and the federal system required juvenile offenders convicted of certain crimes to be sentenced to life without parole, and mandated that they would spend their entire adult lives in prison without any opportunity for release.[224] For these offenders, many of whom had already spent decades incarcerated, *Miller* provided the only hope they had been given since their sentences became final. After all, how could they continue to serve their life-without-parole sentences, now deemed cruel and unusual punishments, without the kind of sentencing hearings the Court had held were constitutionally required? State post-conviction and federal habeas petitions began to trickle and then pour in as prisoners rushed to meet the applicable statutes of limitations.[225]

In March 2015, the Supreme Court granted certiorari in a new case scheduled to be heard during the October term. Montgomery v. Louisiana, 135 S. Ct. 1546, 1546 (2015). The Court also asked the parties to brief the question of whether the Supreme Court has federal question jurisdiction over Louisiana's decision to not grant retroactive relief through state post-conviction proceedings. *Id.*

---

224 *Miller*, 132 S. Ct. at 2471.
225 Under the Antiterrorism and Effective Death Penalty Act (AEDPA), petitioners whose sentences are final on direct review and who are seeking habeas relief must file within a year of the decision that is the basis for their petition. 28 U.S.C. § 2244(d)(1)(A), (C) (2012). This time period is tolled while the petitioner is properly in state post-

WHAT IS RETROACTIVITY?

A brief history of American retroactivity jurisprudence and an explanation of the current doctrine are required to understand the extent of the confusion caused by *Miller* and the inherent theoretical conflict between the retroactivity doctrine and Eighth Amendment jurisprudence. Current retroactivity doctrine allows for four different options along a prospective/retrospective spectrum that a court may consider when determining how a new rule is to be applied: pure retroactivity, full retroactivity, selective perspectivity, and pure perspectivity.[226] Federal retroactivity doctrine, which, for the most part, dictates state retroactivity doctrine,[227] has moved

---

[226] Pure retroactivity means that the new legal rule is applied to all cases, whether on collateral or direct review. Full retroactivity means that the rule is applied to all cases not final on direct review. Selective prospectively means the rule is applied to the case announcing the new rule as well as all cases from that time forward (and sometimes selected cases filed before that date). Pure prospectively restricts the application of the rule to the cases filed only after the date the new legal rule was announced. Courts may also choose a hybrid of these four methods. *See* Paul E. McGreal, *A Tale of Two Courts: The Alaska Supreme Court, the United States Supreme Court, and Retroactivity*, 9 ALASKA L. REV. 305, 307 (1992) (describing these options).

[227] *But see* Danforth v. Minnesota, 552 U.S. 264, 281–82 (2008) (stating that federal law does not limit the state courts' authority to provide retroactive remedies even if a rule is deemed non-

around the spectrum throughout history, with separate, complex rules emerging to govern retroactivity in civil and criminal law.[228] The complexities and inconsistencies once drove Justice Harlan to comment that the Supreme Court's retroactivity doctrine was "almost as difficult to follow as the tracks made by a beast of prey in search of its intended victim."[229] Given the wide reach of the doctrine, this Note discusses only retroactivity as applied to criminal law.

Although *Teague v. Lane* provides the modern blueprint for the federal courts' retroactivity analysis, earlier cases help illuminate the incentive to limit the retroactive application of criminal case law, which is especially salient for Eighth Amendment decisions. The history of retroactivity doctrine is also crucial to understanding the approach courts took towards Eighth Amendment cases decided pre-*Teague*.

The historical background and factors that comprised previous retroactivity frameworks help illuminate how inapplicable the

---

retroactive under *Teague* because the states are free to give broader retroactive effect to new rules in state conviction proceedings).

228 Note, *Prospective Overruling and Retroactive Application in the Federal Courts*, 71 YALE L.J. 907, 907 (1962) (explaining the principle that "judicial decisions are of their nature retrospective").

229 Mackey v. United States, 401 U.S. 667, 676 (1971) (Harlan, J., concurring in part & dissenting in part).

modern doctrine is in the context of the Eighth Amendment, even from an originalist perspective. For almost two hundred years, United States courts applied the pure retroactivity approach as dictated by the Blackstonian view that judges were not really making law but merely "finding" it.[230] In 1965, the Supreme Court finally confronted the retroactivity question in *Linkletter v. Walker*[231] and determined that a change in law would be applicable to all cases on direct appeal.[232] The Court also found that there was

---

230 Under this theory of the judiciary's role, the old rule represented incorrectly "found" law and thus was never actually valid. *See, e.g.*, Legg's Estate v. Comm'r, 114 F.2d 760, 764 (4th Cir. 1940) ("Decisions are mere evidences of the law, not the law itself; and an overruling decision is not a change of law but a mere correction of an erroneous interpretation."); 1 WILLIAM BLACKSTONE, COMMENTARIES *69–70; JOHN CHIPMAN GRAY, THE NATURE AND SOURCES OF THE LAW 93 (2d ed. 1921) ("The Law . . . is identical with the rules laid down by the judges, but those rules are laid down by the judges because they are the law, they are not the Law because they are laid down by the judges; . . . judges are the discoverers, not the creators, of the Law."); Kermit Roosevelt III, *A Little Theory Is a Dangerous Thing: The Myth of Adjudicative Retroactivity*, 31 CONN. L. REV. 1075, 1082 (1999) (noting that the very "concept of retroactivity is a relative newcomer to our jurisprudence" since retroactive application was historically the norm).

231 *See* 381 U.S. 618, 622 (1965) (considering whether the Fourth Amendment exclusionary rule of *Mapp v. Ohio*, 367 U.S. 643 (1961), applied to state convictions that at the time had been final on direct review).

232 Cases are considered final on direct appeal after all trial proceedings and direct appeal proceedings, and the Supreme Court either denies a petition for certiorari or issues a decision. *Compare* Johnson v. New Jersey, 384 U.S. 719, 726–27 (1966) (departing from the statement in *Linkletter* and holding that the three-part test applied equally to criminal cases on direct review), *with* Griffith v. Kentucky, 479 U.S. 314, 322 (1987) (determining

no concrete principle guiding the collateral effect of a subsequent new rule.[26] The Court balanced the conflicting reliance and equity principles at play and created a three pronged test for determining retroactivity: the purpose of the new rule, the reliance placed on the old rule, and the effect of retroactive application on the administration of justice.[233] The justifications behind this approach were fundamentally abandoned with the emergence of the *Teague v. Lane* framework, which governs modern retroactivity analysis.

In 1989, a plurality of the Supreme Court in *Teague v. Lane* departed from the *Linkletter* test and held that new rules of criminal procedure do not apply retroactively to cases that had become final on direct review at the time the new rule was decided.[234] Particularly relevant

---

that failing to apply a constitutional rule to criminal cases on direct review was a constitutional violation, given the Article III "cases and controversies" requirement that federal courts must apply their understanding of the law as the case comes before them). *Linkletter*, 381 U.S. at 627.

233 *Id.* at 629; *see also* Stovall v. Denno, 388 U.S. 293, 297 (1967) (describing the three-part balancing test to be employed in each case: "(a) the purpose to be served by the new standards, (b) the extent of the reliance by law enforcement authorities on the old standards, and (c) the effect on the administration of justice of a retroactive application of the new standards"). Commentators have argued that the *Linkletter* test favored reliance interests over equity principles as government reliance is examined by both the second and third factors and equity is not taken into consideration at all. McGreal, at 310–11.

234 *See* Teague v. Lane, 489 U.S. 288, 296 (1989) (determining the retroactivity of the rule announced in *Batson v. Kentucky*, 476 U.S. 79 (1986)). The *Teague* plurality's retroactivity analysis was endorsed by a majority of the Court and applied to capital cases later that same year. Penry v. Lynaugh, 492 U.S. 302, 314 (1989).

to the thesis of this Note is the justification provided by the Court for this new bright-line retroactivity test: The Court cited equitable treatment of similarly situated defendants,[235] comity and federalism in determining the proper scope of habeas review and the "principle of finality which is essential to the operation of our criminal justice system." The Court then discussed the considerations of cost, reliance, judicial intrusion, and the frustrations of state courts when prisoners were given the ability to upset finalized convictions. According to several Justices, the change in retroactivity was needed to both simplify the retroactivity test and protect the states' interest in finality.

The Court decided that a case announces a new rule when it breaks new ground or imposes a new obligation on the states, or, in other words, if the result was not dictated by precedent when the defendant's conviction became final.[236] The Court also described two exceptions to the general rule against collateral retroactivity. First, new legal rules that place "certain kinds of primary, private

---

The *Teague* plurality left unchanged the *Griffith v. Kentucky* determination that new rules applied retroactively to all cases not yet final on direct review. 479 U.S. 314, 328 (1987).

235 *See Teague*, 489 U.S. at 305 (explaining that announcing new rules in collateral cases and later limiting their retroactive effect has led to disparate treatment). The plurality felt it could fix this inequity by treating retroactivity as a threshold question. *Id.*

236 *See* John Blume & William Pratt, *Understanding* Teague v. Lane, 18 N.Y.U. REV. L. & SOC. CHANGE 325, 340 (1991) (discussing the contradiction in the two definitions of "new rule" in *Teague*).

individual conduct beyond the power of the criminal law-making authority to proscribe" and, second, rules that are "implicit in the concept of ordered liberty."[237] Later cases elaborated and clarified these exceptions to distinguish between substantive and procedural rules: Substantive rules generally apply retroactively, but procedural rules must [238] be "watershed rules of criminal procedure."[239] The

---

[237] *Teague*, 489 U.S. at 307 (citing Mackey v. United States, 401 U.S. 667, 692 (1971) (Harlan, J., dissenting)).

[238] *See* L. Anita Richardson & Leonard B. Mandell, *Fairness over Fortuity: Retroactivity Revisited and Revised*, 1989 UTAH L. REV. 11, 23 (1989) (explaining how and why it took the Court more than twenty years to articulate that the *Linkletter* rule is "as fundamentally arbitrary and indefensible today as it was in 1965"); Benjamin P. Cooper, Comment, *Truth in Sentencing: The Prospective and Retroactive Application of* Simmons v. South Carolina, 63 U. CHI. L. REV. 1573, 1590 (1996) (detailing the multiple motivations driving *Teague*: the states' interests in finality, economic benefits, and incentivizing trial and appellate courts to apply the correct constitutional standards).

[239] Schriro v. Summerlin, 542 U.S. 348, 352 (2004). The *Summerlin* Court also emphasized that the set of rules that would meet the second exception was "extremely narrow." *Id.* at 352. The Supreme Court has never found a claim that fits within the second exception. *See, e.g.*, Caspari v. Bohlen, 510 U.S. 383, 396 (1994) (finding the second exception inapplicable to the rule prohibiting double jeopardy in noncapital sentencing procedures); Gilmore v. Taylor, 508 U.S. 333, 345 (1993) (finding the second exception inapplicable to the rule that homicide instructions denied due process in permitting a jury to convict for murder instead of voluntary manslaughter without considering whether the killing was in the heat of passion); Sawyer v. Smith, 497 U.S. 227, 244 (1990) (finding the second exception inapplicable to the rule that the Eighth Amendment bars imposition of a death sentence by a jury that has been led to falsely believe that responsibility lies somewhere else); Saffle v. Parks, 494 U.S. 484, 495 (1990) (finding the second exception inapplicable to the rule that in a capital sentence hearing, it violates the Eighth

plurality in *Teague* also stated that the retroactivity of any decision should be treated as a threshold issue—thus, the Court should only announce a new rule when the rule would be applied retroactively to the defendant (whether on direct or collateral review) and all those similarly situated.[240] As explained further the articulated concerns for finality and simplicity driving the formulation of the modern framework are fundamentally incompatible with the promise of the Eighth Amendment.

Amendment to provide jury instructions that tell the jury to avoid any influence of sympathy).

240 *See Teague*, 489 U.S. at 300 ("Retroactivity is properly treated as a threshold question, for, once a new rule is applied to the defendant in the case announcing the rule, evenhanded justice requires that it be applied retroactively to all who are similarly situated."). While the plurality characterized the threshold test as part of the holding, four justices continued to support the historic approach of announcing a new rule before deciding its retroactive effect. *Id.* at 319 & n.2 (Stevens, J., concurring in the judgment); *id.* at 339 & n.7 (Brennan, J., dissenting). Justice White did not address the timing issue in his concurrence. *Id.* at 316–17.

REQUIREMENTS FOR FEDERAL HABEAS CORPUS RELIEF AND SUCCESSIVE PETITIONS

In 1996, Congress passed the Antiterrorism and Effective Death Penalty Act (AEDPA),[241] which severely limited the availability of relief through federal habeas corpus petitions.[242][243] Under AEDPA, a federal court ruling on an original petition for federal habeas relief by a state prisoner may not grant it unless the defendant has exhausted state post-conviction remedies and the state court

---

241 Antiterrorism and Effective Death Penalty Act of 1996, Pub. L. No. 104-132, 110 Stat. 1214 (1996).

242 *See* Bryan A. Stevenson, *The Politics of Fear and Death: Successive Problems in Capital Federal Habeas Corpus Cases*, 77 N.Y.U. L. REV. 699, 735–36 (2002) (discussing the collateral effects AEDPA has had on the opportunity for state and federal prisoners to raise claims in habeas actions as to the conditions of their confinement or method of execution).

243 U.S.C. § 2254(d)(1) (2012). A similar provision for federal prisoners is found in 28 U.S.C. § 2255 (2012) (allowing that a prisoner, under custody, claiming the right to be released upon qualifying grounds, "may move the court which imposed the sentence to vacate, set aside or correct the sentence"). Under § 2255, the qualifying grounds require "that the sentence was imposed in violation of the Constitution or laws of the United States, or that the court was without jurisdiction to impose such sentence, or that the sentence was in excess of the maximum authorized by law, or is otherwise subject to collateral attack . . . ." *Id.*

adjudication "resulted in a decision that was contrary to, or involved an unreasonable application of, clearly established Federal law, as determined by the Supreme Court of the United States." On its face, this provision would require that the Supreme Court explicitly determine the retroactivity of all their decisions before state prisoners are entitled to relief through federal habeas proceedings. Furthermore, if the prisoner one has already filed a petition for federal habeas review, the circuit court may only grant him leave to file a successive petition if it is a claim not yet raised and "the applicant shows that the claim relies on a new rule of constitutional law, made retroactive to cases on collateral review by the Supreme Court, that was previously unavailable." Again, the requirement for successive petitions seems to indicate that the Supreme Court must rule on a decision's retroactive effect before federal habeas relief may be granted. In *Tyler v. Cain*, a Supreme Court plurality seemingly endorsed this reading of AEDPA;[244] however, the case law suggests that lower courts have afforded collateral relief in many cases where the Supreme Court has not ruled on the retroactive applicability of its decisions, especially when

---

244 *See* 533 U.S. 656, 663 (2001) ("The new rule becomes retroactive, not by the decisions of the lower court or by the combined action of the Supreme Court and the lower courts, but simply by the action of the Supreme Court.").

retroactivity under the *Teague* framework is uncontested.²⁴⁵²⁴⁶ For both original and successive petitions, the petitioner must file within a year of the decision under which he seeks relief. While AEDPA seems to be a significant obstacle to implementing a presumption of retroactivity, in this context it presents only a minor inconvenience.²⁴⁷

---

245 A more common approach of the lower courts is to determine whether the Supreme Court *would* find a decision retroactive if the case were in front of them, rather than ask if the Supreme Court *already has* declared it retroactive.

246 U.S.C. § 2244(d)(1)(A), (C) (2012).

247 S. Ct. 2455 (2012). On an evening in 2003, fourteen-year-old Evan Miller and a friend smoked marijuana and played drinking games with an adult neighbor. *Id.* at 2462. When the neighbor fell asleep, they stole his wallet. *Id.* The neighbor woke up and tried to stop them, but they hit him repeatedly with a baseball bat. *Id.* Later, they set two fires in order to cover up the evidence of their crime. *Id.* The neighbor died from smoke inhalation and his injuries from the baseball bat. *Id.* The jury found Miller guilty of murder in the course of arson, which statutorily carries a mandatory minimum of life without parole. *Id.* at 2462–63. The Alabama Court of Criminal Appeals affirmed his conviction and his sentence in 2010 and the Alabama Supreme Court denied review. *Id.* at 2463. The Supreme Court granted certiorari on his appeal from the state court determinations, and thus his case was heard on direct review. *Id.*

RETROACTIVITY IN EIGHTH AMENDMENT CASE LAW

The federal and state responses to *Miller* reveal a fundamental conflict between the historical Eighth Amendment presumption of retroactivity and the retroactivity analysis under current doctrine. This Note aims to resolve that conflict by arguing that the Supreme Court should institute a presumption of retroactivity for Eighth Amendment decisions. This conflict has remained hidden, in part, because the Supreme Court in the past has very rarely intervened in punishment outside the context of death.[248]

This Part provides a summary of Eighth Amendment jurisprudence through the lens of retroactivity and illustrates how the question of

---

[248] *See* Woodson v. North Carolina, 428 U.S. 280, 305 (1976) (plurality opinion) ("[T]he penalty of death is qualitatively different from a sentence of imprisonment, however long, [as d]eath in its finality, differs more from life imprisonment than a 100-year prison term differs from one of only a year or two."). *But see* Graham v. Florida, 560 U.S. 48, 82 (2010) (finding juvenile life-without-parole sentences for nonhomicide offenders unconstitutional). Because the Court framed the rule in *Graham* as a categorical decision, it did not present the same conflict as *Miller*.

retroactive application of these cases has always been answered affirmatively. This jurisprudence has created a long-held, but unarticulated, presumption of retroactive application.[249] A

---

[249] U.S. CONST. amend. VIII. The phrase "cruel and unusual punishments" first appeared in the English Bill of Rights in 1689 in response to the sentencing practices of royal judges during the reign of King James II. Anthony F. Granucci, *"Nor Cruel and Unusual Punishments Inflicted:" The Original Meaning*, 57 CAL. L. REV. 839, 840 (1969); *see also* Solem v. Helm, 463 U.S. 277, 285 n.10 (1983) ("There can be no doubt that the Declaration of Rights guaranteed at least the liberties and privileges of Englishmen."); John F. Stinneford, *The Original Meaning of "Unusual": The Eighth Amendment as a Bar to Cruel Innovation*, 102 NW. U. L. REV. 1739, 1759 (2008) ("[The English] Bill of Rights . . . was designed to limit the arbitrary exercise of the monarch's prerogative power."). The first application of the provision was retroactive. An Anglican clerk named Titus Oates had been convicted of perjury in 1685 and sentenced to a fine of two thousand marks, pillorying four times a year, life imprisonment, and to be whipped "from Newgate to Tyburn." Trial of Titus Oates (K.B. 1685), 10 COBBETT'S COMPLETE COLLECTION OF STATE TRIALS 1079, 1315–17 (T. Howell ed., 1811). The court may have believed it was sentencing Oates to be"scourged to death" with this sentence. 2 THOMAS BABINGTON MACAULAY, THE HISTORY OF ENGLAND FROM THE ACCESSION OF JAMES THE SECOND, 62 (Longmans, Green, & Co. 1897). After the Bill of Rights was enacted in 1689, Oates petitioned Parliament for a release from his judgment and the House of Commons passed a bill to release him, finding that the cruel punishments imposed on Oates were beyond the bounds of both the common law and the Bill of Rights. 10 HC Jour. 247 (1689).

Almost a century later, James Madison placed a proscription against "cruel and unusual punishments" in the Bill of Rights he drafted and the language ultimately became part of the Eighth Amendment. *See* Jeffrey D. Bukowski, Comment, *The Eighth Amendment and Original Intent: Applying the Prohibition Against Cruel and Unusual Punishments to Prison Deprivation Cases Is Not Beyond the Bounds of History and Precedent*, 99 DICK. L. REV. 419, 420–21 (1995) (discussing the historical progression of the

discussion of the Eighth Amendment's historical evolution also reveals the original purposes and understandings of the ban on cruel and unusual punishment that guides courts in practical implementation of the Supreme Court's recent decisions. I will also describe some of the conflicted state and federal answers to the question of whether *Miller* applies retroactively to illustrate how courts applying the *Teague* framework misunderstand the implications of the retroactivity question in the Eighth Amendment context.

---

inclusion of the phrase "cruel and unusual punishment" in the American Bill of Rights).

EVOLVING STANDARDS OF DECENCY AND PROPORTIONALITY REVIEW

In 1910, the Supreme Court in *Weems v. United States* [250] rejected for the first time the proposition that the Eighth Amendment reached only punishments that were inhumane, barbarous, or torturous.[251] Through this case, the Court both broadened the scope of the Eighth Amendment to include considerations of proportionality, and explicitly rejected the eighteenth-century conception of cruelty as a basis for cruel and unusual

---

[250] 217 U.S. 349, 381 (1910) (finding a sentence of fifteen years of hard labor while chained at the ankles and wrists for the crime of falsifying a public document unconstitutional). The Court noted the English origins of the text but concluded that the Framers "intended more than to register a fear of the forms of abuse that went out of practice with the Stuarts" and insisted that the Amendment was "not fastened to the obsolete but may acquire meaning as public opinion becomes enlightened by a humane justice." *Id.* at 372–73. In contrasting Weems' sentence to the lighter sentences available for more serious offenses, the Court concluded that it was cruel and unusual. *See id.* at 381 (finding the sentence "exhibit[ed] a difference between unrestrained power and that which is exercised under the spirit of constitutional limitations formed to establish justice").

[251] Note that *Teague* was decided in 1989 and thus was not the framework used to determine the retroactivity of *Furman* or any of the individualized sentencing cases discussed below with the exception of *Sumner*.

punishments.²⁵² This broadened scope of protection was embraced and applied by the Court in later cases to both categories of criminal offenders²⁵³ and types of sentencing power.²⁵⁴ This original understanding of the Eighth Amendment mandates that retroactive application was central to the Framers' formulation of the prohibition against cruel and unusual punishments—it would be impossible to actively impose a torturous method of punishment after it was declared cruel and unusual.²⁵⁵

---

252 *See* Mary Sigler, *The Political Morality of the Eighth Amendment*, 8 OHIO ST. J. CRIM. L. 403, 407 (2011) ("After canvassing various interpretations of the Clause, the Court insisted that the Eighth Amendment 'is not fastened to the obsolete but may acquire meaning as public opinion becomes enlightened by a humane justice.'") (internal citations omitted).

253 *See* Robinson v. California, 370 U.S. 661, 667 (1962) (declaring the state criminalization of narcotic drug addiction "cruel and unusual" and thereby unconstitutional). *Robinson* also incorporated the Eighth Amendment's ban on cruel and unusual punishments into the Fourteenth Amendment's Due Process Clause, rendering it applicable to the states as well as the federal government. *Id.* at 666.

254 *See* Trop v. Dulles, 356 U.S. 86, 102–04 (1958) (plurality opinion) (invalidating a sentence of expatriation for the crime of wartime desertion). The Court found that while expatriation did not constitute torture in the traditional sense of physical brutality, it amounted to "a form of punishment more primitive than torture . . . destroy[ing] for the individual the political existence that was centuries in the development." *Id.* at 101. As a result, expatriation was inconsistent with the "dignity of man" and consensus of civilized nations underlying the Eighth Amendment. *Id.* at 100.

255 *See* Wilkerson v. Utah, 99 U.S. 130, 135–36 (1878) ("Difficulty would attend the effort to define with exactness the extent of the constitutional provision . . . but it is safe to affirm that

The majority of the Court has declined to adopt a robust proportionality review doctrine for all criminal sentencing, and instead has carved out categorical exceptions for death sentences and juvenile life-without-parole sentences.[256] The formulation of the Court's "evolving standards of decency" test has fluctuated in its individual application, but is generally measured by an assessment of contemporary values both through objective indicia[257] and the independent judgment of the judiciary[258].Several of the Eighth Amendment cases discussed in the next section are examples of the Court's application of the test to specific types of offenders and sentences and are targeted to answering the retroactivity question.

---

punishments of torture . . . and all others in the same line of unnecessary cruelty, are forbidden . . . .");

256 See Harmelin v. Michigan, 501 U.S. 957, 997–1002 (1991) (Kennedy, J., concurring in part and concurring in judgment) (concluding that the Eighth Amendment contains only a "narrow proportionality principle," that "does not require strict proportionality between the crime and sentence" but rather "forbids only extreme sentences that are 'grossly disproportionate' to the crime"). *Id.* at 1001.

257 These indicia are primarily patterns of jury decision making and trends in legislation. Occasionally, the Court also engages in an international comparison. See Graham v. Florida, 560 U.S. 48, 80 (2010) ("There is support for our conclusion in the fact that, in continuing to impose life-without-parole sentences on juveniles who did not commit homicide, the United States adheres to a sentencing practice rejected the world over.").

258 See Gregg v. Georgia, 428 U.S. 153, 173 (1976) (quoting *Trop*, 356 U.S. at 100) (noting that the judicial responsibility to exercise independent judgment is to ensure that the punishment is consistent with "the dignity of man").

The Supreme Court in *Miller* draws on two lines of Eighth Amendment precedent in its analysis of the constitutionality of mandatory juvenile life-without-parole sentences.[259] Each of the cases in both lines of case law has been retroactively applied by the lower courts, implying that until *Miller* there was an assumed presumption of retroactivity. This Note's proposition that an articulated presumption is the appropriate solution in the Eighth Amendment context is bolstered by an understanding of the reasons for the "silent" presumption of retroactivity. Since some of these cases were decided under pre-*Teague* case law, it is important to understand the evolving justifications for restricting retroactivity under the doctrine.

The cases mandating individualized sentencing in the death penalty context were all decided before *Teague v. Lane* replaced the increasingly convoluted *Linkletter* triad. After the Supreme Court in *Furman v. Georgia* found that the imposition of the death penalty in the cases before them was a violation of the Eighth and Fourteenth Amendments, the states and Congress were required to rewrite their capital sentencing schemes in order to comport with the requirement that the death penalty not be administered in an arbitrary or capricious manner.[260] In the four years that passed between *Furman*

---

[259] *See* Miller v. Alabama, 132 S. Ct. 2455, 2466 (2012) (detailing the line of categorical exemptions and individualized sentencing requirements that informed the Court's decision).

[260] Furman v. Georgia, 408 U.S. 238, 239–40 (1972) (finding two death sentences for homicide and one for rape unconstitutional

and the Court's subsequent ruling on the constitutionality of capital sentencing mechanisms, there was effectively a moratorium on the death penalty and those individuals already on death row were not executed. Hence, it was widely understood, although not litigated, that *Furman* applied retroactively and those with finalized convictions would benefit from any changes in state or federal sentencing practices.[261] On July 2, 1976, the Supreme Court

---

although the Justices in the majority did not produce a controlling opinion as to what the violation was).

261 *See* Woodson v. North Carolina, 428 U.S. 280, 301 (1976) (plurality opinion) (invalidating a statute mandating death sentence for first-degree murder); *Gregg*, 428 U.S. at 196–98 (finding a death penalty scheme requiring additional evidence of an aggravating factor valid); Proffitt v. Florida, 428 U.S. 242, 247–53 (1976) (validating a statute requiring the jury to weigh mitigating factors against statutory aggravating factors); Jurek v. Texas, 428 U.S. 262, 276–77 (1976) (ruling a narrow definition of capital murder and scheme which required jury to consider "special issues" valid); Roberts v. Louisiana, 428 U.S. 325, 332–37 (1976) (invalidating a mandatory death penalty scheme for five categories of first degree murder). In upholding the Georgia, Florida, and Texas statutes and striking down the North Carolina and Louisiana statutes as unconstitutional, the Court effectively banned any sentencing scheme that made the death penalty mandatory for certain crimes. *See, e.g., Woodson*, 428 U.S. at 301 (finding that the first-degree murder death penalty statute in North Carolina "departs markedly from contemporary standards respecting the imposition of the punishment of death and thus cannot be applied consistently with the Eighth and Fourteenth Amendments' requirement that the State's power to punish 'be exercised within the limits of civilized standards'" (quoting *Trop*, 356 U.S. at 100). The Court further held that "in capital cases the fundamental respect for humanity underlying the Eighth Amendment . . . requires consideration of the character and record of the individual offender and the circumstances of the particular offense as a constitutionally indispensable part of the process of inflicting the penalty of death." *Id.* at 304.

explained in five separate decisions the requirements for states to constitutionally sentence offenders to death. Anyone put to death after this date would have to be sentenced under a constitutional scheme, regardless of when his or her conviction was final.

In *Lockett v. Ohio*[262] and *Eddings v. Oklahoma*,[263] the Court emphasized that, constitutionally, a sentencer in capital cases could not be precluded from considering as a mitigating factor any information about the defendant or the circumstances of the crime. In doing so, it differentiated the requirements of capital sentencing from noncapital sentencing due to the irreversible nature of the punishment of death. Both *Lockett* and *Eddings* were retroactively applied by the lower courts.[264] In *Sumner v. Shuman*, the Court effectively slammed a door already closed in *Woodson v. North Carolina*[265] and found unconstitutional a statute mandating the death penalty for an inmate convicted of murder while serving a life sentence.[266] *Sumner* was a case decided on collateral review two

---

262 438 U.S. 586 (1978).

263 455 U.S. 104 (1982).

264 *See, e.g.*, Dutton v. Brown, 812 F.2d 593, 599 n.7 (10th Cir. 1987) (noting that "retroactive application" of *Lockett* is mandatory); Songer v. Wainwright, 769 F.2d 1488, 1489 (11th Cir. 1985) (applying *Lockett* retroactively); Harvard v. State, 486 So. 2d 537, 539 (Fla. 1986) (same); Shuman v. Wolff, 571 F. Supp. 213, 216 (D. Nev. 1983) (applying the rule from *Eddings* retroactively), *aff'd*, 791 F.2d 788 (9th Cir. 1986), *aff'd sub nom.* Sumner v. Shuman, 483 U.S. 66 (1987).

265 428 U.S. 280 (1976).

266 483 U.S. 66 (1987).

years before *Teague*, but later courts using the *Teague* framework applied it retroactively.[267] In drawing on the individualized sentencing line of precedent in *Miller*, the Court has crossed the divide it previously created between capital and noncapital cases and, for the first time, found the Constitution requires individualized sentencing for a sentence less than death. Because all individual sentencing cases were decided before *Teague*, courts have never had to determine how modern retroactivity doctrine conflicts with the presumption of retroactive application these new rules carry.

Under *Teague*'s rationale, if the Supreme Court decides a case on collateral review, there is an indication that the decision meets either the substantive rule exception or the watershed procedural rule exception, and therefore applies to all those similarly situated.[268] One line of cases the Court draws on in *Miller* discusses the

---

[267] See Campbell v. Blodgett, 978 F.2d 1502, 1512–13 (9th Cir. 1992) (determining merits of Sumner claim in case that became final two years before *Sumner* was decided); Thigpen v. Thigpen, 926 F.2d 1003, 1005 (11th Cir. 1991) (noting death sentence set aside on *Sumner* grounds in federal habeas corpus case); McDougall v. Dixon, 921 F.2d 518, 530–31 (4th Cir. 1990) (determining merits of *Sumner* claim in a case that became final four years before *Sumner* was decided). On a meta-theoretical level, the courts applying *Teague* to *Sumner*—a case that was decided two years before the new retroactivity framework was instituted—were retroactively applying retroactivity. Of course, this could also be explained by courts applying the retroactivity framework applicable at the time of the claim brought under *Sumner* instead of the one applicable at the time of *Sumner* itself.

[268] See Teague v. Lane, 489 U.S. 288, 307–10 (1989) (adopting Justice Harlan's two exceptions to the general rule of non-retroactivity in cases on collateral review).

categorical exemptions of certain groups of people from specific types of punishment— namely, capital punishment or life-without-parole sentences.[269]

In 2005, the Supreme Court held that the Eighth Amendment did not permit death sentences for any juvenile defendant, even those guilty of first-degree murder. *Roper v. Simmons* was decided on collateral review, on appeal from state post-conviction proceedings, and was retroactive when announced.[270] Since the procedural posture of the case determined the retroactivity question, the courts were generous in providing relief in post-conviction review and many state prisoners did not have to resort to federal habeas review.[271]

---

[269] Miller v. Alabama, 132 S. Ct. 2455, 2463–64 (2012). In these cases, the Court has found a mismatch between the culpability of a class and the harshness of the penalty inflicted based on either the nature of the offense or the characteristics of the offender.

[270] *Roper*, 543 U.S. at 559–60. This reasoning could also be extended to the companion case in *Miller, Jackson v. Hobbs*, which was also decided on collateral review of state post conviction proceedings. 132 S. Ct. at 2461.

[271] *See* Lee v. Smeal, 447 F. App'x 357, 359 n.2 (3d Cir. 2011) (vacating retroactively a death sentence for a seventeen-year-old offender and replacing with two consecutive life sentences); Loggins v. Thomas, 654 F.3d 1204, 1209–10 (11th Cir. 2011) (explaining the Alabama Court of Criminal Appeals determination that *Roper* applied retroactively to cases finalized on direct review); Horn v. Quarterman, 508 F.3d 306, 307–08 (5th Cir. 2007) (discussing the Texas Court of Criminal Appeals decision to grant relief to the seventeen year-old defendant and commute his death sentence to life); LeCroy v. Sec'y, Fla. Dep't of Corr., 421 F.3d 1237, 1239–40 (11th Cir. 2005) (stating that the Florida Supreme Court vacated the seventeen-year-old defendant's death

For cases decided on direct review, the lower federal and state courts have had to decide the retroactivity question for themselves. *Atkins v. Virginia*, the case on which Sullivan[272][273] based his state post conviction petition, addressed the constitutionality of executing a defendant who was mentally retarded.[274] *Atkins* was decided on direct appeal,[275] yet due to the categorical nature of the rule announced and the Supreme Court cases previously addressing the

---

sentence based on an application of *Roper* in state post-conviction review).

272 Sullivan v. Florida, 560 U.S. 181 (2010). Originally the companion case to *Graham v. Florida*.

273 U.S. 304 (2002). In *Atkins*, the Court held that those who are mentally retarded are "categorically less culpable than the average criminal" and thus the execution of such an individual violates the Eighth Amendment. *Id.* at 304.

274 Roper v. Simmons, 543 U.S. 551 (2005). The Court found that offenders under eighteen were across-the-board less culpable than adults and thus could not under any circumstances be punished by a death sentence. *Id.* at 569–71. This applied an extension of the Court's plurality opinion in *Thompson v. Oklahoma* which set the minimum age for the death penalty at sixteen and stressed that the "reasons why juveniles are not trusted with the privileges and responsibilities of an adult also explain why their irresponsible conduct is not as morally reprehensible as that of an adult." 487 U.S. 815, 835 (1988). Note that in *Thompson* the Court set aside the death sentence for a fifteen-year-old offender but Justice O'Connor concurred on narrower grounds. Graham v. Florida, 560 U.S. 48, 60–61 (2010) (holding that juveniles could not be sentenced to life without parole for non homicide offenses).

275 *See id.* at 310 (providing the procedural history of *Atkins v. Virginia*).

retroactivity issue,[276] lower courts have consistently applied the rule retroactively to cases on collateral review.[277][278]

Three years after *Roper*, the Supreme Court held in *Kennedy v. Louisiana* that the Eighth Amendment did not permit a sentence of death for a rapist, even when the victim is a child, who did not also commit homicide. In doing so, the Court turned from *Roper*- and *Atkins*-type analyses categorically exempting the offender to a study of the crime committed, and determined that offenses not resulting in death, while they may be horrific, are categorically less deserving of capital punishment.[279] Retroactivity was not litigated after this case as only Kennedy and one other offender (out of more than three thousand total) were on death row for a no homicide.[280] It is clear,

---

276 *See, e.g.*, Penry v. Lynaugh, 492 U.S. 302, 339–40 (1989) (holding that the execution of a prisoner with the mental capacity of a seven-year-old did not violate the Eighth Amendment). The Court ruled unanimously that the first *Teague* exception "prohibited a certain category of punishment for a class of defendants because of their status or offense" but rejected the claim on the merits. *Id.* at 330.

277 *See* Ochoa v. Sirmons, 485 F.3d 538, 540 n.2 (10th Cir. 2007) (accepting the State's concession that the Supreme Court had anticipatorily made the case expressly retroactive in *Penry v. Lynaugh*); *In re* Holladay, 331 F.3d 1169, 1172–73 (11th Cir. 2003) (collecting cases in which *Atkins* has been found retroactive); *In re* Morris, 328 F.3d 739, 740 (5th Cir. 2003) (same).

278 554 U.S. 407 (2008).

279 *Id.* at 421; *see also* Coker v. Georgia, 433 U.S. 584, 600 (1977) (barring the use of death as a penalty for the rape of an adult woman).

280 *See* Kennedy v. Louisiana, DEATH PENALTY INFO. CTR., http://www.deathpenalty info.org/kennedy-v-louisiana-no-07-

however, that had a court needed to determine *Kennedy*'s retroactivity, it would have fallen into the first *Teague* exception as a categorical decision that placed beyond the power of the state punishment by execution for offenders convicted of rape but not homicide.[281]

Atkins, *Roper*, and *Kennedy* all introduced categorical exemptions to imposition of the death penalty, but in 2010 the Supreme Court extended the categorical proportionality review to life-without parole sentences imposed on juvenile offenders for no homicide crimes.[282] In *Graham*, the majority, over the objections of Chief Justice Roberts in his concurrence,[283] established a rule that a punishment of life without parole for the class of juvenile offenders convicted of nonhomicide offenses was cruel and unusual under the Eighth Amendment. The Court both relied and expanded on the scientific and developmental research used in *Roper* to find that

---

343 (last visited June 12, 2015) (listing total number of death sentences for sexual assault of a child by states). Although six states allowed the death penalty for child rape, only Louisiana actually imposed it on offenders. *Id.*

281 *See Kennedy*, 554 U.S. at 421 (holding death sentences unconstitutional for those who rape but do not kill a child); *see also Teague*, 489 U.S. at 307 (citing Mackey v. United States, 401 U.S. 667, 692 (1971) (Harlan, J., dissenting) (providing the definition of a categorical decision).

282 Graham v. Florida, 560 U.S. 48, 100–03 (2010) (Thomas, J., dissenting).

283 *See id.* at 86–91 (Roberts, C.J., concurring) (urging the Court to adopt a case-by-case proportionality analysis instead of a categorical ban).

juveniles were categorically less culpable than adult offenders. In likening life-without-parole sentences to death for juvenile offenders, the Court seemed to extend the "death is different" Eighth Amendment framework[284] to include the notion that "kids really are different."[285] *Graham* was a case on direct review,[286] but the majority's decision to frame the question as a substantive categorical exemption rather than an additional procedural burden has led lower courts to apply the decision retroactively.[287]

---

284 *See Roper*, 543 U.S. at 568 (explaining how historically the Eighth Amendment has applied to death sentences with "special force" because death is the "most severe punishment").

285 Marsha Levick, *Kids Really Are Different: Looking Past Graham v. Florida*, 87 CRIM. L. REP., 664, 664–65 (2010) (describing the extension of the Eighth Amendment framework beyond *Graham*).

286 *Graham*'s companion case, *Sullivan v. Florida*, was on collateral review but the Supreme Court dismissed the writ as "improvidently granted" due to a state procedural bar. 560 U.S. 181, 182 (2010). The defendant in *Sullivan* could later use the holding in *Graham* to obtain retroactive relief. *See EJI Client Joe Sullivan's Death-in-Prison Sentence Overturned by United States Supreme Court's Ruling*, EQUAL JUSTICE INITIATIVE (May 17, 2010), http://www.eji.org/node/394 ("Joe Sullivan . . . will now use the new rule established in *Graham* to obtain a new sentence that . . . provides a 'realistic opportunity to obtain release.'")

287 *See, e.g.*, *In re* Evans, 449 F. App'x 284, 284 (4th Cir. 2011) (per curiam) (noting the government "properly acknowledged" *Graham* applies retroactively on collateral review); Kleppinger v. State, 81 So. 3d 547, 550 (Fla. Dist. Ct. App. 2012) (applying *Graham* on collateral review); Manuel v. State, 48 So. 3d 94, 97 (Fla. Dist. Ct. App. 2010) (same); State v. Dyer, 2011-1758, p. 3 (La. 11/23/11); 77 So. 3d 928, 930 (same); Rogers v. State, 267 P.3d 802, 804 (Nev. 2011) (noting that the district court properly applied *Graham* retroactively). It is interesting to note that had the majority adopted Chief Justice Roberts's mechanism

DIMINISHED STATE INTEREST IN FINALITY

In *Teague*, a plurality of the Supreme Court moved away from the case-by-case approach of the *Linkletter* balancing test and established a bright-line rule for collateral non-retroactivity of new rules of criminal law, subject to two exceptions. As justification for the new retroactivity analysis, the Court cited equitable treatment of similarly situated defendants,[288] the "interests of comity . . . in determining the proper scope of habeas review,"[289] and the "principle of finality which is essential to the operation of our criminal justice system."[290] In constructing the new analysis,

---

[288] Teague v. Lane, 489 U.S. 288, 305 (1989) (explaining that announcing new rules in collateral cases and later limiting their retroactive effect has led to disparate treatment). The plurality felt it could fix this inequity by treating retroactivity as a threshold question. However, it is clear from the cases discussed in Part II.B *supra* and *Miller* itself that the Court has not consistently done so.

[289] *Id.* at 308.

[290] *Id.* at 309. The Court also discussed the considerations of cost, reliance, judicial intrusion, and the frustrations of state courts when prisoners were given the ability to upset convictions final on direct review. *Id.* at 310.

retroactive availability of new rules was curtailed to address these concerns.

This Note is not meant to be a general criticism of the *Teague* standard or its ability to meet the stated concerns,[291] but a critique based on the diminished value of these interests in the Eighth Amendment context—specifically, the principle of finality and the costs imposed on the State.[292] In no sense does retroactively applying a decision based on the Cruel and Unusual Punishment Clause upset the finality of criminal *convictions*. Instead, these decisions necessarily affect criminal punishments, i.e., *sentencing*. In the categorical cases, new rules required that states commute capital sentences to life-without-parole sentences—as in *Roper* and *Atkins*—and life without-parole sentences to life or "term-of-years" sentences—as in *Kennedy* and *Graham*. No retrial or prosecution by the State was necessary, simply judicial resentencing. For individualized sentencing cases and *Miller*, the procedural framing of the rule does slightly increase the State's burden as the resentencing hearings must incorporate all mitigating evidence on

---

291 For a detailed critique of the *Teague* decision and its progeny, see generally Blume & Pratt, *supra* note 34, at 326 (claiming that the rule announced in *Teague* did not contribute to the goals of simplifying retroactivity analysis or protecting the State's interest in finality).

292 A fear that prisoners were inundating courts with multiple appeals similarly influenced AEDPA's federal habeas reforms. *See* Stevenson, *supra* note 40, at 711–22, 728 (explaining the "hidden" narrative driving AEDPA);

behalf of the defendant. Still, the upset to the interest in finality goes to the sentence and not the conviction, and no retrial is required. The cost and inconvenience to the State, while present, is minimal compared to the concern underlying *Teague*'s limitation—the reopening of the conviction itself. Applying *Teague* allows states to differentiate between the categorical and the individualized sentencing rules, finding the former retroactive and the latter non-retroactive, though both require merely resentencing processes.

Applying the presumption of retroactivity to all Eighth Amendment decisions will actually increase judicial efficiency and lower costs since the issue will no longer have to be litigated extensively in state and federal courts. The presumption would additionally serve the equity purpose that the *Teague* plurality tried to address by making retroactivity a threshold question. Having a stated presumption of retroactivity for any new rules under the Eighth Amendment would end the state-by-state disparities (apparent in the aftermath of *Miller*) that concerned the Justices in *Teague*.

While the states' interest here in non-retroactivity is diminished, the defendants' interest in retroactivity is greatly heightened. Fundamental to the Eighth Amendment is the protection of human dignity[293] and the premise that "even the vilest criminal remains a

---

293 *See* Gregg v. Georgia, 428 U.S. 153, 173 (1976) (upholding the revised Georgia criminal sentencing procedures).

human being possessed of common human dignity."²⁹⁴ The underpinnings of the Constitution's Cruel and Unusual Punishment Clause are distinctively moral—both in what is moral for a prisoner to endure, and what is moral for a state to inflict.²⁹⁵ Therefore, while other new rules may enact procedures to ensure fairness and accuracy in criminal proceedings, rules based on the Eighth Amendment enhance our commitment to decency and resistance to inhumanity.²⁹⁶ Until *Miller*, Eighth Amendment decisions either specifically addressed the death penalty and were deemed retroactive, or were captured by *Teague*'s substantive rule exception. With *Miller*, the Court has shown its willingness to extend the sentencing requirements of the Eighth Amendment beyond the death context. For now, this principle has only applied to juvenile offenders. The presumption of retroactivity should not be thwarted just because the *Miller* rule requires individualized sentencing for lifetime incarceration instead of the death penalty. *Teague* artificially separates the cohesive Eighth Amendment promise by distinguishing between substantive and procedural manifestations of the same moral assurance. As shown in the Eighth Amendment case law, deeming a new rule "procedural" ensures it

---

294 Furman v. Georgia, 408 U.S. 238, 273 (1972) (Brennan, J., concurring).
295 *See* Sigler, at 406 (suggesting that moral considerations lie at the heart of Eighth Amendment analysis).
296 *See id.* at 405 (arguing that the evolving standards of decency test highlights important liberal-democratic values).

will not be retroactively applied under *Teague* given that no procedural change has ever been found to meet the "watershed" standard. *Teague* also does not consider the underlying purpose of creating a new rule, and in this context incorrectly allows for the state interest in finality and cost to outweigh basic human dignity.

The *Teague* analysis does not account for the realities of Eighth Amendment decision-making since the "new rule" distinction is incompatible with the "evolving standards of decency" test. Under the Supreme Court's framework, a punishment or sentencing scheme is found to be cruel and unusual if it is against contemporary societal values—measured by patterns of jury verdicts and legislative enactments as well as the Justices' own independent judgment.[297] The test is grounded in both objective indicia of what the national consensus actually is, and the Justices' independent belief in what it should be.[298] The Court is creating or announcing a

---

297 *See* Roper v. Simmons, 543 U.S. 551, 561–63 (2005) (describing cases where the Court decided that capital punishment is cruel and unusual where the defendant is under the age of sixteen at the time of the crime or "mentally retarded" because of evolving standards of decency); Graham v. Florida, 560 U.S. 48, 61 (2010) (explaining the Court's two-part approach, which is grounded in "objective indicia of society's standards, as expressed in legislative enactments and state practice" and the Court's Eighth Amendment precedents).

298 For a critique of this approach, see, for example, *Roper*, 543 U.S. at 608 (Scalia, J., dissenting) (calling the Court's reliance on "evolving standards" and evidence of a "national consensus" wrong); Stinneford, , at 1746 (2008) (advocating the view that Eighth Amendment interpretation should focus on "longstanding traditions").

new *legal* rule to match the *moral* rule they believe is already in play. However, the plurality in *Teague* characterized new rules in a purely legal sense.[299] Thus, although Eighth Amendment decision-making is based precisely on discovering and concretizing existing moral rules into legal ones, the *Teague* analysis labels them as "new" and limits their retroactive application on this basis. However, given the justification for distinguishing between old and new rules—protecting states' reliance interest—enforcing a standard which gives defendants the benefit of rules supported by legal precedent, but not by widespread national moral consensus, makes no sense. Defendants have just as much, if not more, at stake when the basis of the unconstitutionality of their punishment is from the national collective conscience as when it is from existing legal precedent.

Also irreconcilable with the Eighth Amendment's protection against cruel and unusual punishment is *Teague*'s placement of finality at conviction.[300] When the new rule concerns trial proceedings, it may make sense to have a case become "final" on conviction so that the

---

299 A rule is new if it "breaks new ground or imposes a new obligation on the States or Federal government" or "if the result was not *dictated* by precedent existing at the time the defendant's conviction became final." *Teague*, 489 U.S. at 301. Existing moral rules could arguably be left out of the first description of a "new rule" but are captured by the second, since they are in no way dictated by existing legal precedent. *Id.*

300 *Id.* at 310 (stating that convictions are final once a defendant's direct appeals are complete).

states will not be obligated to reopen and retry cases indefinitely. But in the Eighth Amendment context, the finality of a conviction and sentencing does not coincide with the actual infliction of the punishment. Put another way, placing the barrier at conviction allows the state to implement or continue to implement a cruel and unusual punishment after it is declared unconstitutional. Through this lens, when a new rule concerns the constitutionality of a punishment, the application is always prospective until the time the punishment is completed.[301] The fact that the completion of punishment is exceedingly clear-cut in the death penalty context—at the time of execution—may explain why individualized sentencing cases in the pre-*Teague* era were simply assumed to be retroactive.

Two illustrations are useful in illuminating this point. If the Supreme Court on December 31, 2025 declares that certain types of torturous punishments, such as stun belts[302] or water boarding,[303] are against

---

[301] Which in the capital or life-without-parole case would be the defendant's death through either state-inflicted or natural causes.

[302] *See* Julian Borger, *US Prisons 'Use Electric Shock Belts for Torture,'* THE GUARDIAN (June 8, 1999, 20:41 EDT), http://www.theguardian.com/world/1999/jun/09/julianborger (discussing stun belts as a form of torture).

[303] President Obama banned the use of waterboarding in January 2009. Exec. Order No. 13,491, 3 C.F.R. § 3(b) (2009); Ewen MacAskill, *Obama: 'I Believe Waterboarding Was Torture, and It Was a Mistake,'* THE GUARDIAN (Apr. 29, 2009; 22:23 EDT), http://www.theguardian.com/world/2009/apr/30/obama-waterboarding-mistake.

the country's evolved sense of decency and thus cruel and unusual, this decision would constitute a new rule of criminal law. It would be unthinkable for the federal or state governments to continue to use stun belts or water boarding after the decision was issued, whether or not a particular defendant's conviction had been final on that date.[304] For the state to do so would be an active, visible infliction of an unconstitutional punishment. Similarly, a moratorium on the death penalty put in place by the Supreme Court in *Furman* was lifted, with certain procedural restrictions, by *Gregg v. Georgia* and its companion cases in 1976. For the states to execute those on death row whose convictions and death sentences were final pre-*Furman* in the intervening years would be inconceivable given that the Supreme Court had said the process by which those defendants were sentenced to death was unconstitutional. When the moratorium was lifted in *Gregg*, the state would not execute these same prisoners before providing the constitutionally-mandated procedural protections for capital sentencing. To do otherwise would be implausible and bring a barrage of media and public outrage.

---

304 For the purposes of this illustration, I lay aside the fact that a total ban against a form of punishment would be encompassed under *Teague*'s categorical exception. The result would be the same if the Supreme Court instead required individualized sentencing and limited the use of stun belts and water boarding to the rarest of cases.

The only differences between the examples above and *Miller* is the type of state action that is required to impose the punishment. In the case of the death penalty and torture, the State would have to actively and visibly inflict an unconstitutional form of punishment in order to deny retroactive relief, which they are understandably unwilling to do. The point of finality here is located not at conviction, but at the time of the execution or torture. In the case of life-without parole sentences, the State is not required to act to impose the punishment, but instead can opt to do nothing and let the prisoner continue to serve his sentence until death. This is both less visible and easier to justify on moral grounds, which is why non-retroactivity becomes an option. However, the effect is the same—after the date at which a punishment has been declared cruel and unusual, the State continues to impose it based on the arbitrary line of finality placed at conviction. In the punishment context, finality should be found at the culmination of the punishment being served—death instead of conviction for capital and life-without-parole sentences—which can be implemented through a presumption of retroactivity for both capital and noncapital sentences.

THE NEW FRAMEWORK AND ITS PRACTICAL IMPLEMENTATION

Given the history of Eighth Amendment jurisprudence and the relative dearth of Supreme Court rulings on retroactivity in this area, it seems there is already an existing, unspoken presumption of retroactivity. The decisions post-1989 concerning cruel and unusual punishments have all been retroactively applied without question, or made to fit into one of the *Teague* exceptions by the lower courts. *Miller*, on the other hand, points to a new doctrinal development expanding individualized sentencing requirements outside the death penalty context. Therefore, an articulation of the presumption of retroactivity could be highly beneficial in the future.[305] Even within the strict requirements of AEDPA, there are several ways the presumption can be put into practice, even if the Supreme Court does not resolve the question of *Miller* retroactivity. First, states and Congress usually have to write new legislation after Eighth Amendment decisions, altering their

---

305 Additionally, it is unclear whether the individualized sentencing cases pre-1989 would have been applied retroactively if they were subject to *Teague*.

sentencing schemes to bring them up to constitutional muster.[306] The legislative bodies can easily insert retroactivity clauses into these new bills and avoid costly litigation and adjudication. Second, since retroactivity is not constitutionally dictated, the state courts have the option to go beyond what *Teague* allows.[307]

State courts, as seen in the post-*Miller* muddle, can, and sometimes do, provide relief through state post-conviction proceedings. If they recognize an articulated presumption of retroactivity for Eighth Amendment rules, state courts would have guidance in making these determinations and little reason for denying petitions. AEDPA requirements would not even be brought into question if prisoners did not have to rely on federal habeas as a final resort. Finally, although AEDPA seems to explicitly require that the Supreme Court make a rule retroactive before a circuit court can grant leave for a prisoner to file a successive petition, this requirement has not been consistently applied by the lower courts. The more common practice

---

306 *See, e.g.*, H.B. 152, 2013 Leg., Reg. Sess. (La. 2013) (setting a mandatory minimum of thirty-five years for juvenile defendants sentenced to first- and second-degree murder and requires that they complete educational and job training programs before being eligible for parole). The Act leaves life-without-parole sentences as an option. *Id.*

307 Danforth v. Minnesota, 552 U.S. 264, 282 (2008) (stating that federal law does not limit the state courts' authority to provide retroactive remedies even if a rule is deemed non-retroactive under *Teague* because the states are free to give broader retroactive effect to new rules in state conviction proceedings).

is for lower courts to discern whether the Supreme Court would have found a decision to be retroactive and deny or grant a petition on that basis. Applying a presumption of retroactivity will allow these decisions to be made in a more consistent, equitable, and methodological manner. The Supreme Court would only have to address the retroactivity question in the rare, perhaps nonexistent, instance the Court makes a new rule regarding cruel and unusual punishments that it did *not* want retroactively applied. If the Supreme Court substantively resolves the question of *Miller* retroactivity by articulating a presumption of retroactivity for Eighth Amendment decisions, it will provide a framework for state courts and legislatures and lower federal courts moving forward.

Norval Morris, Towards Principled Sentencing, 37 Md. L. Rev. 267 (1977)

Government is not always beneficent, your response tells me. Nor is the wish to do social good always the immediate prelude to its achievement. Nowhere are these truths more evident than in the governmental task of sentencing convicted criminals, a task to which the author directs attention today. So much seems to be expected of the criminal sentence: crime reduction, deterrence coupled with clemency, a deserved punishment linked to that insightful individualization of punishment which fosters self regeneration. The sentencing decision is complex, difficult, and of fundamental importance; yet we lack a common law of sentencing. The purposes to be achieved by sentencing are not agreed upon, nor are our procedures. A mixture of motives has led us astray: on one hand, an exaggerated belief in the deterrent efficacy of punishments; on the other, an excessive faith in the possibility of coercively transforming the criminal into a law-abiding citizen. Both deterrence and reform have failed us: deterrence, because our limited capacity to catch, convict, and sentence the guilty fails to fulfill the threat of punishment; reform, because coercive reform is no business of the criminal law. When the criminal law enters that business, it tends to corrupt its legitimate purposes, achieving neither justice nor social protection.

It is obvious as the author states that he is not going to solve these mysteries today. Some of man's earliest writings deal with the proper equation between crime and punishment; the subsequent literature is enormous; no transcendent truths will emerge today. But it may be possible, at a time of ferment in sentencing reform, to offer some ideas relevant to legislative, judicial, and academic discussions of the various current proposals for sentencing reform - that, certainly, is my purpose.

The first insight the author submits for consideration is that sentencing reform is unlikely substantially to reduce crime or juvenile delinquency. The press and its willing acolytes, the politicians, frequently promise substantial diminution of crime and juvenile delinquency through manipulation of court procedures and a hardening of sentencing practice. Be not deceived. There is much wrong with the American criminal justice system but its leading defect is not, as the tabloids suggest, the sentimentality of the judiciary. In many days' marches through the criminal courts of this country, the author found few bleeding-hearted judges; they tend, in terms of physiognomy, to the prognathous jaw and the hard nose, far from characteristic of the sentimental softies the press describes.

The allegation of too lenient sentencing by the judge is an irrelevancy, a distraction from the systemic difficulties that beset sentencing practice, particularly in the crowded urban courts of this country. The public has been led to expect too much of the criminal justice system generally and grossly too much from sentencing reform. The criminal justice system controls the largest power the government exercises over its citizens and is of central constitutional importance, but its reform, if consonant with a due respect for human rights and fundamental freedoms, will make no more than relatively small differences in the incidence of crime and juvenile delinquency. These phenomena respond to deep social, cultural, and political currents beyond the substantial influence of the criminal justice system.

The system cannot itself rectify social inequities; but it certainly should not exacerbate them, as it does now. The system cannot end the poverty that persists amidst conspicuous plenty, it cannot abolish racial discrimination in a country dedicated to the equality of man, it cannot solve the diverse problems of our criminogenic society. Does that mean that sentencing reform is unimportant? Not at all. It is of crucial importance. All that the author is struggling to refute are those unrealistic expectations which have long blighted criminal law reform. The author tries to be clear about what can reasonably be expected of sentencing reform: first what cannot and then what can be expected.

The shadow that crime now casts across the face of America is unlikely to be much reduced until, in the 1980's, changes in the age and distribution of our population give us surcease. We have gathered together our minority, ill-educated youth, underemployed and vocationally untrained, in pockets of desolation in our larger cities. Welfare programs have contributed to the breakdown of the families of the poor and have helped make criminals of their children. A drug culture powers crime in the ghetto. A plague of handguns has turned domestic conflicts into gun battles and has eased the path of the socially pressured towards street crime. Crime in the suites gives moral leadership to crime in the streets. A multiplicity of police forces burdened by excessive minor service and regulatory duties achieves exiguous clearance rates of crime.

The jails, the courts, and the prisons are overcrowded: in particular, the prison population swells in its inadequate and ancient premises. It is most unlikely that sentencing reform will make a substantial inroad on these criminogenic realities. Let me give an example. Van Dine, Dinitz and Conrad have recently conducted an experiment [308] to test statistically whether mandatory incapacitated sentences - as advocated by Wilson, Van den Haag and others [309] - would substantially reduce violent crimes. The most stringent option they tested, a five-year net mandatory term for any adult convicted of a felony, would have reduced crime in the area studied by only four percent. Such a sentencing system would, of course, be nullified and modified in practice, and the payoff would be even less. [310] And more realistic, less draconic, mandatory sentences are likely, I shall argue, to have even less effect on the crime rate.

What, then, can sentencing reform achieve? The journey will not be short nor the results easy of achievement but, in my view, we can reasonably expect a small but measurable reduction of crime and juvenile delinquency and, at least equally important, the emergence of a principled, evenhanded, effective yet merciful common law of sentencing, consistent with human rights and just freedoms,

---

308 Van Dine, Dinitz & Conrad, The Incapacitation of the Dangerous Offender: A Statistical Experiment, 14 J. RESEARCH IN CRIME & DELINQ. 22 (1977).

309 See, e.g., E. VAN DEN HAAG, PUNISHING CRIMINALS: CONCERNING A VERY OLD AND PAINFUL QUESTION (1975); A. WILSON, THINKING ABOUT CRIME 198-209 (1975).

310 The deterrent efficacy of such sentences was, of course, not measured.1977]

competent to deter crime, outline minimum behavioral standards, and better protect society against its in group predators.

The author hopes by what the diplomats affectedly call a tour d'horizon, to throw some light on certain key issues in the emergence of such a common law of sentencing. But there yet remain a few necessary preliminary points.

There are at least two aspects to the emergence of a principled jurisprudence of sentencing: purposive and procedural. The purposes of punishment are too often considered apart from the machinery of their achievement, and the awkward squalor of reality thus banished. Though artificial isolation of a topic is often necessary for its elucidation, in this instance principle and procedure are so deeply intertwined that our only hope of moving towards principled sentencing lies in new procedures and, in particular, in the better control of charge and plea bargaining and the wiser distribution and control of sentencing discretion between the legislature, the judge, and the administrator than now obtain.

A new procedural synthesis is essential to principled sentencing. The author hopes to move towards some clarity as this lecture grinds relentlessly on. In a relatively recent book, [311] the author to isolate sentencing purposes from sentencing procedures and offered an answer to the question "Why should a convicted criminal be

---

[311] N. MORRIS, THE FUTURE OF IMPRISONMENT (1974).

imprisoned?"; this seemed to the author a practical way to contribute to a jurisprudence of sentencing. It is suggested two guiding principles: the principle of parsimony, whereby the least restrictive (punitive) sanction necessary to achieve defined social purposes should be imposed; and the principle of desert, whereby no sanction should be imposed greater than that which is "deserved" by the crime, or series of crimes, for which the offender is being sentenced. With the advancement of dogmatic views on the proper application of special and general deterrence and on predictions of future dangerousness in the imposition of punishments.

These issues are important and relevant to the emergence of a common law of sentencing, but the author prefers to focus on their relationship to sentencing procedures and, in particular, to the questions of who should impose sentence on the criminal and under what legislative, judicial, and administrative limitations.

One of the compelling reasons for this necessary synthesis of purpose and procedure is the diversity of crime. Punitive purposes appropriate to homicide are less relevant to petty larceny certainly the mixes of purposes to be achieved are different. Incest, drunken driving, bank robbery, and embezzlement present substantially different social problems which are unlikely to be effectively addressed by any simple hierarchy of punishment aims. The necessary operative complexity will have to be found in sentencing processes capable of mediating those differences.

And further, discretion in punishment, an inevitably necessary element as we shall see, may properly be differently exercised at different levels of the criminal justice system. Given that a prosecutor exercises a sentencing discretion in his decision to accept a plea of guilty to a lesser charge than that for which he might possibly obtain a conviction, his discretion to do so is properly less circumscribed than that of a judge imposing sentence after a jury trial and conviction. The latter is more public: the deterrent and educative functions of the criminal law weigh more heavily. Hence, we face problems not only of the proper ends of punishment but also of the appropriate distribution of punitive discretion.

Finally, before a series of current sentencing problems is listed and commented upon, the author addresses the question why sentencing has now caught the public eye. The books on sentencing [312] flow to such an extent that my brilliant colleague, Franklin Zimring, has been moved to publish "A Consumers' Guide to Sentencing Reform.'" The legislative proposals and reforms multiply, from California [313] to Maine. [314] Statutory sentencing reform is in the wind, and Congress now girds itself for the consideration of at least two important reform initiatives, the

---

312 CAL. PENAL CODE §§ 1170.0-1170.6 (West Cum. Supp. 1977).

313 ME. REV. STAT. ANN. tit. 17-A, §§ 1151-1156, 1201-1206, 1251-1254, 1301-1305 (Supp. 1975).

314 S. 181, 95th Cong., 1st Sess., 123 CONG. REC. 406 (daily ed. Jan. 11, 1977).

Kennedy Bill [315] and the Hart-Javits Bill." Why the flurry? Why the present ferment? Many reasons, but one in particular merits present comment.[316] A false dichotomy long concealed the tensions in sentencing policy which have now become manifest. We long conducted the debate in polar terms. One was either for punishment and deterrence or one was for treatment and reform. In those simplistic days, before we recognized the inadequacies in our rehabilitative and reform models of the criminal process, the diversity in sentencing, the disparities in the treatment of apparently like cases, was explained either by the incompetence or inefficiency[317] of the judiciary in properly individualizing punishment to adjust the needs of social defense to the rehabilitation of the offender.

Francis Allen's essay on the rehabilitative ideal' [318] attracted enormous support. In the same year that Allen's book of essays was published, 1964, the author found that he was arguing that "power

---

315 S. 204, 95th Cong., 1st Sess., 123 CONG. REC. 556 (daily ed. Jan. 12, 1977).
316 E.g., D. FOGEL, WE ARE THE LIVING PROOF: THE JUSTICE MODEL FOR CORRECTIONS (1975); M. FRANKEL, CRIMINAL SENTENCES: LAW WITHOUT ORDER (1973); A. VON HIRSCH, DOING JUSTICE, THE CHOICE OF PUNISHMENTS, REPORT OF THE COMMITTEE FOR THE STUDY OF INCARCERATION (1976).
317 F. ZIMRING, MAKING THE PUNISHMENT FIT THE CRIME: A COMSUMERS' GUIDE TO SENTENCING REFORM (1977).
318 F. ALLEN, Legal Values and the Rehabilitative Ideal, in THE BORDERLAND OF CRIMINAL JUSTICE: ESSAYS IN LAW AND CRIMINOLOGY 25 (1964).

over a criminal's life should not be taken in excess of that which would be taken were his reform not considered as one of our purposes."' [319] In 1964 that was not an obvious proposition. It can hardly be argued against now. Many studies and a legion of commentators, culminating perhaps in the overstatement of Martinson's swiftly accepted view that "nothing works"' [320] have forced reconsideration of the traditional polar argument between the punishers and the treaters.

The problems of just sentencing are now seen to be more complex; the pervasive unjust disparity of sentencing more difficult of remedy. Suggestions of a simple balance between encompassed harm and deserved punishment receive widespread support; though they too, as the author argues misleadingly simplify the problem and will not achieve the larger equities at which we aim. The balance between desert, deterrence, the educative effects of punishment on the community, a due respect for human rights and minimum dignities, the lasting constraints of clemency and charity, and the existing and likely continuing inadequacies of our understanding of man and his place in society, the whole compounded by the great diversity of crime and the paucity of resources we allocate to its just

---

319 N. MORRIS & C. HOWARD, STUDIES IN CRIMIINAL LAW 175 (1964).

320 Martinson, What Works? Questions and Answers About Prison Reform, 35 THE PUBLIC INTEREST 22 (1974). See also D. LIPTON, R. MARTINSON & J. WILKS, THE EFFECTIVENESS OF CORRECTIONAL TREATMENT: A SURVEY OF TREATMENT EVALUATION STUDIES

control, make up a problem insoluble by simplistic solutions like mandatory minimum sentences or legislatively fixed sentences.[321]

And all this complexity is, in the authors view, pressing on us now for two reasons: an increasing recognition of the serious impact crime has on life in this country, and a clearer perception that the criminal law is an unlikely engine for coercing man to the good life or for coercing the criminal to social conformity. The astonishingly swift passage of the years has not shaken the author's faith in this conclusion; the data on unjust sentencing disparity have indeed become quite overwhelming and will, convince anyone who will take the time to study them. The author draws attention to just a few recent studies illustrative of both judicial and parole board disparity in sentencing.

In a recent experiment in the Federal Second Circuit, [322] all forty-three of the active federal trial judges in that circuit and seven senior trial judges rendered sentences on twenty identical cases set forth in presentence reports. [323] There was a wide range of disagreement among the judges regarding appropriate sentences for identical

---

[321] Morris, Sentencing Convicted Criminals, 27 AUSTL. L. J. 186 (1953).

[322] A. PARTRIDGE & W. ELDRIDGE, THE SECOND CIRCUIT SENTENCING STUDY: A REPORT TO THE JUDGES OF THE SECOND CIRCUIT (1974).

[323] Each presentence report contained information regarding the crime, whether the guilty verdict followed a plea or trial, prior record, age, narcotic history, family background, etc.

cases. For example, in one case the sentences varied from three to twenty years, and in another from probation to seven and one-half years. Furthermore, even after eliminating the extremes of the distribution, substantial disagreement persisted. Absence of consensus was found to be the norm. In a study of sentencing councils, Diamond and Zeisel found that such councils have a relatively small effect on the very large disparity present in the system. [324] Sentencing councils attempt to reduce sentencing disparity by requiring each judge to discuss with his fellow judges the cases on which he is to pass sentence. Before the council discussion, disparity averaged around forty-five percent of the mean severity of sentence in the Eastern District of New York and about thirty-seven percent in the Northern District of Illinois; the disparity reduction effected by the councils was only about four percent. In a recent study of sentences in federal courts throughout the country, Tiffany, Avichai and Peters found substantial variation in sentences that related to such apparently unprincipled factors as: type of trial - whether by bench or jury; type of counsel - whether retained or appointed (but only in bench trials); race of defendant (but only where defendant had no prior record). [325]

---

[324] Diamond & Zeisel, Sentencing Councils: A Study of Sentence Disparity and Its Reduction, 43 U. CHI. L. REV. 109 (1975).

[325] Tiffany, Avichai & Peters, A Statistical Analysis of Sentencing in Federal Courts: Defendants Convicted After Trial, 1967-68, 4 J. LEGAL STUD. 369 (1975).

The discovery of such unprincipled disparity took many students of the criminal justice system by surprise, but, in retrospect, it should not have. Sentencing in America has not been guided by any apparent principles, and certainly not by legislatively enunciated principles. It has been left to the caprices of judges with various characters and training, working under pressures of crowded court dockets, and to the vagaries of changing judicial and public attitudes towards crime and punishment. No considered or routine procedure guides the imposition of sentence, nor have generally accepted criteria been established. The judge need not give reasons for his decision nor explain it to the convicted criminal. Because disparity flows from lack of principle and absence of modulating procedures, one wonders if perhaps the individualized attentions of parole boards can achieve a larger equity. But parole boards are even less constrained than judges by controlling principles or procedures. Studies similar to the judicial sentencing studies discussed above have found unjust disparity also in the decision to release on parole. 326

It is important to understand that these sentencing studies try to hold constant those individual qualities, both in the criminal and his social setting, which are thought to justify individualization of punishment and thus to explain its variation from the norm. Several

---

326 E.g., Heinz, Heinz, Senderowitz & Vance, Sentencing by Parole Board: An Evaluation, 67 J. CRIM. L. & CRIMINOLOGY 1 (1976).

decades of research seem to me to have clearly demonstrated not the existence of sentencing disparity possibly justified by the needs of individualized sentencing, but rather the existence of gross sentencing disparity not capable of being so justified.

The currently fashionable leap to the automatic equality of fixed term sentencing, the sentence determined by the severity of the crime and modulated only slightly by defined aggravating and mitigating circumstances found by the judge to influence the deserved punishment, is clearly understandable as a pendulum reaction to our long-prevailing sentencing anarchy. But it is, the author believes, a mistake; and for two reasons. First, as will be seen when we discuss legislatively fixed term sentencing, such systems are incapable of encompassing the subtleties of crime-to-criminal relationships essential to just sentencing. Secondly, equality in punishment is not an absolute principle; it is a value to be weighed and considered among other values, no more; and there can be just sentences in which like criminals are not treated alike. [327]

---

[327] This is a long argument which I have developed elsewhere at burdensome length, N. Morris, Punishment, Desert and Rehabilitation, in (7) EQUAL JUSTICE

FAILURE OF FEDERAL AND STATE JUDGES IN ARIZONA TO BRING THE RULE OF LAW TO SENTENCING ENCOURANGES VINDICTIVE LEGISLATION

John S. Martin, Jr., Cruel and Usual: Sentencing in the Federal Courts Jurist in Residence, 26 Pace L. Rev. 489 (2006)

Judge John S. Martin gave the following speech quoted verbatim in part:

If I were to tell you that every day federal judges are ordering that the dominant hand of drug offenders be cut off, you would no doubt all be appalled and feel a need to do something about such inhumanity. While no one's hand is being cut off, every day in the federal court's judges are imposing such harsh sentences that the defendant would probably prefer to have his or her hand cut off. In a speech to the American Bar Association two years ago Justice Kennedy said of our sentencing system,[328] "Our resources are misspent, our punishments too severe, our sentences too long.'" Let's start with the statement that our sentences are too long. I do not

---

[328] Associate Justice Anthony M. Kennedy, Speech at the American Bar Association Annual Meeting (Aug. 9, 2003), available at http://www.supremecourtus. gov/publicinfo/speeches/sp_08-09-03.html.

question that there are those who should be in jail for long periods of time and some who should never see the light of day outside prison.

The problem with our current criminal sentencing system is that it does not draw distinctions between the serious offender who deserves the maximum possible sentence and others whose crimes are less serious or whose involvement is less substantial. When I started out as an Assistant to the United States Attorney in the early sixties, there was a five-year mandatory drug sentence that was considered extremely harsh. It was rare to see a defendant, other than someone prosecuted under that mandatory statute, receive a sentence of five years in jail. Today, there are 168,000 prisoners in the federal system and approximately 68% of them are serving sentences of five years or more. [329]Twenty percent of those prisoners are serving sentences in excess of fifteen years and 12% are serving sentences over twenty years. What is interesting is that only 3.2% of those incarcerated in our federal penitentiaries have been convicted of murder, kidnapping or aggravated assault, which we normally think of as the crimes that would warrant such severe sentences.

---

329 Up-to-date statistics regarding the number of federal prisoners can be found at The Federal Bureau of Prisons, http://www.bop.gov/index.jsp (last visited Jan. 6, 2006).

Let me give you a few examples of how overly severe sentences are being applied to low level violators. About a year before I retired, I was presiding at a pretrial conference in a criminal case. I asked the Assistant U.S. Attorney to outline the proof against the defendant. He said that this defendant, who was an addict, sat on a stoop on a public street and when people would come up and ask where they could get crack, he would tell them of the apartment in which the other defendants were selling crack. Because he did this, from time to time the crack dealers would give him some crack for his own use. I asked what the guideline sentence was. The answer was that, because the defendant had prior convictions for street level sales of drugs, under the guidelines the sentence was approximately sixteen years, and there also was a mandatory minimum sentence of twenty years that could apply.

Another example is found in an opinion I wrote in a case entitled United States v. Williams. [330] In that case, the defendant had been involved in the sale of twenty-nine grams of heroin to an undercover police officer. He did not play a major role in transaction, although he was present when the heroin was delivered and helped count the money paid by the undercover police officer. Williams, who was then in his early twenties, presented the picture of a typical defendant in the federal narcotics cases. He was raised by a single mother in the projects in the Bronx. He began using marijuana at the

---

330 78 F. Supp. 2d 189 (S.D.N.Y. 1999).

age of ten. At the age of nineteen he was convicted in state court of having sold two envelopes of heroin to an undercover officer. Nine months later, he was convicted for selling a ten-dollar bag of crack to an undercover officer. Approximately two years later, he was arrested for selling crack on the street. Under the Federal Sentencing Guidelines, Williams faced a minimum sentence of twenty-two years.

These two cases provide good examples of sentences which are too long that are regularly being imposed on minor drug violators. However, it is not only the very long sentences that can be too severe. Let me give you two other examples. One of the early cases I tried, involved a single mother of two children who worked at the United States Post Office in downtown Manhattan on the night shift. At approximately 11:30 p.m. one night, she had her break and went to a local bar where she joined two other women from the post office waiting to buy some cocaine for their personal use. When the cocaine dealer came in, they each said that they wanted a twenty-dollar bag. He asked one of them to step outside with him to exchange the money for the cocaine, and the defendant volunteered to do this. She was found guilty of distributing cocaine within a thousand feet of a school, which carried a mandatory one-year prison sentence.

In another case, a woman, who was a Hispanic immigrant, was before me in a case involving food stamp fraud. Her husband had been the leader of a group that had been involved in the purchasing food stamps from welfare recipients for cash and he was sentenced to approximately six years. According to the Government the husband would occasionally bring food stamps home and have his wife stamp them on the back with an endorsement necessary to deposit them. Occasionally he would have her take the food stamps to the bank and deposit them. Although she had three children, one of whom was severely retarded, the guideline for her sentence was 2 1/2 years in jail. While each of the cases I have described involves someone who clearly did something the law prohibits, in none of the cases was the sentence prescribed appropriate. I should tell you that in each of the cases, we were able to work out a more favorable disposition. However, these cases are examples of why there must be discretion in sentencing. Unfortunately, I do not think all judges would have believed that they had the power to depart from the guideline sentences in those cases.

The perception that our sentences are too severe is not simply that of some group of liberal judges. In response to an article published in The New York Times, I received a letter from a judge in the South who described himself as a conservative and said: when I was appointed by President Reagan in the Fall of 1985, I thought my biggest concern in sentencing would be to make sure that hard core criminals were not routinely given lenient sentences. I soon found out, however, that the guidelines, particularly in drug case, are so favorable to the prosecution that I must devote much of my attention to trying not to give harsh sentences where none is required.

One of the things that I have found interesting is the extent to which Court personnel, not directly involved as parties to the litigation, have expressed their concern about the severity of the sentences being imposed in our courts. People like our interpreters and our court reporters have on numerous occasions told me about incidents where they just were shocked by the sentence that was being imposed on a particular defendant. I recall a court reporter telling me that she had just taken a proceeding in which a young man in his twenties had been sentenced to life without parole for a narcotics violation even though there had been no violence associated with his activity. He was in fact a dealer in substantial quantities of narcotics, and deserved a substantial sentence, but putting him away for the rest of life seemed to her and to me an unduly harsh punishment. Several years ago, I visited a women's prison in Texas where I met a well-spoken woman in her twenties who was serving life plus thirty-five years because of her involvement in her boyfriend's crack distribution operation.

You might ask why, if our sentences are so harsh, has there not been More of a public outcry. To a large extent, the answer is found in the population upon whom we are imposing these harsh and cruel sentences. Of the 168,000 prisoners in our federal prisons today, 40% are Black, 32% are Hispanic, and another 3% are Asian or

Native American. [331] While there may be some overlap in the Black and Hispanic populations, I think it is fair to estimate that between 65 and 70% of the federal prison population are minorities. I do not believe that we have a consciously racist criminal justice system. I do believe, however, that because these sentences are imposed on minorities, they do not cause the majority community the concern they would feel, if the defendants were people with whom we identified in a meaningful way.

Several years ago in a speech to the Federal Bar Council in New York, my former colleague, Bob Carter said that if as large a percentage of the White community was being imprisoned as is happening in the Black community, our society simply would not tolerate it and would look more closely at the root causes and do something. I am firmly convinced he is correct. It is not that we are consciously trying to imprison minorities, we simply do not care enough about the problems that minorities face. Let me turn now to Justice Kennedy's statement that our resources are misspent. Two years ago, I visited a federal women's prison in Arizona in which 270 women were incarcerated. There were no prison walls, no barbed wire, nothing that would prevent any of them from leaving the camp. At night between 10:00 p.m. and 6:00 a.m. there was one

---

331 For statistics regarding prison populations by race see the U.S. Department of Justice,
http://www.ojp.usdoj.gov/bjs/welcome.html (last visited Jan. 5, 2006).

Bureau of Prisons employee on duty at that institution. It was a warehouse for women, many of whom were mothers with young children. I asked myself what conceivable good it is doing for society to have most of these women warehoused here while their children are raised in foster homes or by distant relatives. We are just making sure that we repeat the cycle that will lead their children to spend a good part of their lives in our prison system.

There are other ways in which our resources are being misspent on lengthy prison terms for minor violators. Several years ago, the Rand Corporation did a cost benefit analysis of various approaches to our narcotics problem.7 the study concluded that every million dollars spent on incarcerating drug offenders for longer periods of time would result in the decrease of thirteen kilograms of cocaine distributed. However, if you took that same million dollars and, rather than spending it for prison guards and other correctional costs, used it to put more police and drug agents on the street, you would reduce narcotics distribution by twenty-seven kilograms. Even more revealing, the study found that, if you took that million dollars and spent it treating heavy users in narcotic addiction programs, you would reduce cocaine consumption by over one hundred kilograms. Unfortunately, it is easier to run for Congress by saying you voted for harsher mandatory sentences for drug dealers than by saying you voted to allocate more money for drug addiction programs.

Another way to see how our resources are misspent in our sentencing system is to look at the escalation of the cost of imprisonment in the federal system. In 1978, there were 20,000 people in the federal system at a cost of $308 million. Today, there are 168,000 people in federal prison at a cost of over $5 billion. The question that has to be asked: is this vast increase in the amount we are spending incarcerating our fellow citizens having a substantial impact on crime? I suggest that the answer is no. Forty percent of the people in federal prison are there because of narcotics related offenses. However, statistics will show that there has been no diminution in the number of narcotics addicts or narcotics being distributed in this country. Our current sentencing scheme also leads to inefficiency in the war against drugs. We have gotten to the draconian sentences which exist today, because ever since I was an Assistant United States Attorney in the early 1960s, drug enforcement officials would tell Congress that we can win the war on drugs if we increase drug sentences. Time after time, Congress would respond to that argument by increasing the penalties.

However, these harsh penalties are applied without any thought about the level of involvement of the particular defendant in the narcotics distribution scheme. When you fail to distinguish between major and minor violators, you give the law enforcement community the ability to brag about their success in prosecuting narcotics violators. They can testify before Congress and say look, there are 40,000 people who are in federal prison for sentences of over ten years because of their narcotics violations. What is not said is that the incarceration of 95% of those individuals will have no meaningful impact on the number of drugs distributed because those individuals are low level members of narcotics distribution organizations who can be immediately replaced upon their arrest.

It is very easy for drug enforcement officers to go out on the street and arrest addicts selling drugs as in the Williams case. But you end up with somebody doing more than twenty years in jail that was immediately replaced by another addict willing to sell drugs to get some for himself. Drug agents can create impressive statistics by arresting low level drug dealers. It takes a much greater law enforcement effort to prosecute major violators who do not operate openly on the streets. If we simply limited the harsh penalties to major violators, we would be providing the Drug Enforcement Agency with an incentive to concentrate their efforts on major violators, and we would have a way of measuring the success of law enforcement in the war on drugs. I am not opposed to the concept of sentencing guidelines. The Sentencing Reform Act, which established the guideline system, had as its central theme the concept that judges should have guidelines to follow in imposing sentence so that there would be uniformity in sentences. To accomplish this end, the statute set up a panel of experts; a sentencing commission that was charged with the task of setting up guidelines for the sentencing for each violation of federal law. A guideline tells the judge what the sentence should be in a typical case. Thus, judges in California and New York can look at the guidelines to determine the appropriate sentence for the typical drug dealer who sells a kilogram of heroin.

However, there are three factors that have combined to make our sentencing regime unconscionably severe. First, Congress has adopted numerous excessively harsh mandatory minimum sentences, which give the judge no discretion in imposing a sentence. Second, at the time the Sentencing Commission was formed, it was charged with developing a philosophy of sentencing and developing a sentencing system that would fix appropriate sentences for various types of criminal conduct. However, when the Commission attempted to do this, they found that they could not reach a consensus on these major issues. Rather than attempt to use their expertise to set appropriate sentences the Commission simply took an average of the sentences for each type of crime that had been imposed in the past and used that average sentence to establish the guideline for that offense. Thus, the Sentencing Commission, which was established to replace a flawed system, took the average result from that flawed system and adopted that as the guideline for future sentences. Third, the Sentencing Commission felt compelled to fix the guideline sentences to make them consistent with the lengthy mandatory minimum sentences that Congress had mandated for various offenses, particularly narcotics offenses. Since the mandatory minimums are too high the guidelines are also too high. While these problems primarily relate to drug sentences, once drug sentences were set at a high range, there has been a tendency to increase the sentences in white collar cases to avoid the perception of a double standard. Thus, we can now proudly say that we treat white collar defendants almost as unfairly as we treat narcotics defendants.

Justice Kennedy, in his address to the ABA, stated that the guideline sentences are too high and should be revised downward. I enthusiastically agree. Since the guidelines became effective in 1989, the number of people in federal prisons has grown from 47,000 to 168,000. During the last three years I was on the court, I served on the Criminal Law Committee of the Judicial Conference and we worked closely with the Sentencing Commission. I am confident if the Commission had the freedom to set the guidelines without Congressional interference, they would do much to alleviate the harshness of our sentencing system. However, Congress refused to let the Commission do the job it was created to do and continuously attempted to micromanage the work of the Commission.

For example, the Commission did an extensive study of the disparity in sentencing for crack and powder cocaine and found no justification for it. When the Commission considered amending the guidelines to reduce the crack penalties to the level of powder cocaine, it was told by leaders in Congress that if the changes were adopted Congress would overrule them. While some in the defense bar rejoiced at the Supreme Court's decision in United States v. Booker[332] as signaling the end of the rigidity of the sentencing guidelines, I think the joy is unwarranted. Although the Supreme Court said that the guidelines were not mandatory, it said that the sentencing judge must still consider the guideline. This was reiterated by the Second Circuit in United States v. Crosby. [333] I think that the experience since Booker indicates that there has not been a substantial increase in the extent of departures from the guidelines and I do not think that there will be.

If I was given the choice, I would abandon our guideline system entirely and do away with all mandatory sentences. Those who favor sentencing guidelines observe that such guidelines provide a rational basis for ensuring that defendants who commit similar crimes in similar circumstances will receive similar sentences. Since ending unwarranted disparity in sentencing was a principal reason for establishing the guideline system, the first question to be asked is whether experience has shown that this goal has been accomplished. A look at the most recent statistics from the Commission's 2003 Annual Report suggests that the answer to that question is a resounding "no."

---

332 543 U.S. 220 (2005).
333 397 F.3d 103 (2d Cir. 2005).

Peter A. Ozanne, Bringing the Rule of Law to Criminal Sentencing: Judicial Review, Sentencing Guidelines and a Policy of Just Deserts, 13 Loy. U. Chi. L. J. 721 (1982).

The plea for a legislative sentencing policy based upon the theory of just deserts demonstrates again that the reduction of sentence variation depends ultimately upon judgments of value about the proper objectives of criminal punishment. Even with a full array of procedural safeguards, sentence disparity will continue to be a prominent feature of our penal systems unless theories of punishment that condone or conceal variable sentencing treatment are excluded from their sentencing policies. No amount of judicial review can eradicate sentence disparity in a system which openly pursues the crime prevention strategies of deterrence theory at the expense of equal sentencing treatment as a matter of sentencing policy; nor will sentence review assure that like cases will be treated alike in rehabilitative or incapacitated systems where sentences are based upon idiosyncratic decisions allegedly made by firsthand observation or expert judgment.

This plea for a just desert sentencing policy is also based upon a principled, even handed, effective yet merciful Common Law of Sentencing, consistent with human rights and freedoms, competent to the deterrence of crime, the adumbration of minimum standards of behavior and the better protection of society against its in-group predators. The decision-making process in a sentencing guidelines system should be legitimated by public understanding and by governmental checks and balances. If a guidelines system is to accomplish its regulatory function, the criminal justice community and the public must understand the methods it employs and feel confident that the system is being held in check by the processes of government. This is the primary significance of a legislative sentencing policy based upon a theory of just deserts.

Despite doubts about the affirmative case for taking an eye for an eye and a tooth for a tooth, the just deserts concept of proportionate punishment provides a standard that the public can comprehend and that reviewing courts can apply. The concept admittedly lacks precision. However, it grounds a sentencing system in the historical facts of offenses and prior criminal records which can be understood by the average citizen and verified and evaluated by the appellate courts.

By comparison, an incapacitated guideline system focuses on propensities for future criminal conduct and employs a technology that is becoming increasingly incomprehensible to citizens and courts alike. The methodology of categoric risk prediction makes it likely that, without a degree in criminology and a mastery of statistical science, the average citizen will view the allocations of punishment it produces as incoherent and unfair and the average appellate judge will regard the value judgments it requires as technical and final. Such a system presents the prospect of guidelines administrators, without the electoral mandate of legislators or the institutional detachment of judges, making the final, controversial, and unchecked decisions of what is a fair distribution of punishment and a rational allocation of corrections resources.

Adoption of a sentencing guidelines system represents the single most important step in regulating sentencing practices and reducing disparity. The administrative structure of the system, with a sentencing commission as the centerpiece, supplies the same insulation from political whim that has made the parole system a sometimes useful if covert mechanism to standardize sentences. However, this kind of insulation also represents a lack of political accountability that has increasingly proved fatal to systems of pa role. The workings of a guidelines system, with its matrix tables of severity ratings and criminal history scores, too easily conjure up images of the therapeutic state and give rise to claims of "sentencing by computer, [334] to ignore demands for political accountability.

If a sentencing guidelines system is to survive amidst the political pressures and competing objectives of a penal system, it needs the popular support that a comprehensible legislative sentencing policy

---

334 See Jacobs, American Implications of Sentencing by Computer, 4 RUTGERS J. OF COMPUTRFS AND THE LAW 302 (1975).

can bring and the institutional checks that the appellate courts can provide. This kind of political accountability is the ultimate value that a sentencing policy of just deserts and judicial sentence review can promote in the regulation of criminal sentencing.

DUE TO EXCESSIVE SENTENCES IMPOSED BY ARIZONA JUDGES --EXCESSIVE WHEN COMPARAED TO THOSE IMPOSED BY THE FEDERAL SYSTEM, OTHER STATES AND THE INTERNATIONAL COMMUNITY MANDATES APPLYING THE EIGHTH AMENDMENT AND ICCPR

Nancy Gertner, A Short History of American Sentencing: Too Little Law, Too Much Law, or Just Right, 100 J. Crim. L. & Criminology 691 (2010)

In colonial times, and particularly in the period before American independence,[335] juries were de facto sentencers with substantial power. [336]Many crimes were capital offenses. [337]The result was binary—guilty and death, or not guilty and freedom. There were few scalable punishments, or punishments involving a term of years.

---

335 See Michael E. Horowitz & April Oliver, Foreword: The State of Federal Prosecution, 43 AM. CRIM. L. REV. 1033, 1039-40 (2006).

336 See Albert W. Alschuler & Andrew G. Deiss, A Brief History of the Criminal Jury in the United States, 61 U. CHI. L. REV. 867, 869-76 (1994) (reviewing early jury trials); Judge Nancy Gertner, Circumventing Juries, Undermining Justice: Lessons from Criminal Trials and Sentencing, 32 SUFFOLK U. L. REV. 419, 424 (1999).

337 Note, Procedural Due Process at Judicial Sentencing for Felony, 81 HARV. L. REV. 821, 832-33 (1968).

³³⁸This is so because penitentiaries were not common until the end of the eighteenth century. ³³⁹ Jurors plainly understood the impact of a guilty verdict on the defendant because of the relative simplicity of the criminal law and its penalty structure, and often because of the process by which they were selected. They were picked from the rolls of white men with property. Indeed, steps were sometimes taken to secure better qualified people to serve on juries. Juries were hardly representative in the sense that we understand today. ³⁴⁰ The substantive criminal law was the province of the states, and was, for the most part, state common law, often deriving from cases with which the jurors were familiar. ³⁴¹

Like the modern jury, colonial jurors were authorized to give a general verdict without explanation, but unlike the modern jury, the colonial jury was explicitly permitted to find both the facts and the law. ³⁴² If capital punishment were inappropriate, they would

---

338 While Langbein describes this development in terms of the English jury system, his observations apply with special force to the colonial jury. See JOHN H. LANGBEIN, THE ORIGINS OF THE ADVERSARY CRIMINAL TRIAL 64 (2003).

339 SOL RUBIN, THE LAW OF CRIMINAL CORRECTION 27-30 (1973).

340 Douglas G. Smith, The Historical and Constitutional Contexts of Jury Reform, 25 HOFSTRA L. REV. 377, 432 (1996).

341 Lance Cassack & Milton Heumann, Old Wine in New Bottles: A Reconsideration of Informing Jurors about Punishment in Determinate- and Mandatory-Sentencing Cases, 4 RUTGERS J.L. & PUB. POL'Y 411, 439-40 (2007) (citing J.M. BEATTIE, CRIME AND THE COURTS IN ENGLAND, 1660-1800 (1986)).

342 Akhil Reed Amar, The Bill of Rights as a Constitution, 100 YALE L.J. 1131 (1991). As Professor Amar noted: [I]t was widely

simply decline to find guilt, or find the defendant guilty of a lesser crime in order to avoid the penalty of death. No one disparaged this as "jury nullification." Ignoring the law to affect a more lenient

---

believed in late eighteenth-century America that the jury, when rendering a general verdict, could take upon itself the right to decide both law and fact. So said a unanimous Supreme Court in one of its earliest cases (decided before Callender) [Georgia v. Brailsford, 3 U.S. (3 Dall.) 1, 4 (1794)] in language that resonates with the writings of some of the most eminent American lawyers of the age—Jefferson, Adams, and Wilson, to mention just three. Indeed, Chase himself went out of his way to concede that juries were judges of law as well as of fact. Perhaps, however, this concession had to do with the peculiarities of sedition law and its somewhat unusual procedures—driven, it will be recalled, by the struggle between judge and jury. Id. at 1193; see, e.g., R. J. Farley, Instructions to Juries—Their Role in the Judicial Process, 42 YALE L.J. 194, 303 (1932) ("In America by the time of the Revolution and for some time thereafter, the power to decide the law in criminal cases seems to have been almost universally accorded the jury . . . ."); see also David A. Pepper, Nullifying History: Modern-Day Misuse of the Right to Decide the Law, 50 CASE W. RES. L. REV. 599, 609 (2000) (arguing that colonial juries had the right to decide the law as outlined by the Court); cf. Edith Guild Henderson, The Background of the Seventh Amendment, 80 HARV. L. REV. 289 (1966) (distinguishing between civil and criminal juries, and dismissing Brailsford as anomalous). But see Stanton D. Krauss, An Inquiry into the Right of Criminal Juries to Determine the Law in Colonial America, 89 J. CRIM. L. & CRIMINOLOGY 111, 131 (1998) (suggesting that the historical record is not clear).

outcome was well within the jury's role. [343] In fact, several colonies explicitly provided for jury sentencing. [344]

Thus, in the colonial division of labor, juries had a preeminent role. [345]There was no need for a priori punishment standards or rules, because there was, for the most part, a single punishment. Penal philosophy, at least as a formal matter, was retributive. There was little national federal law, even after independence. Most criminal

---

[343] Blackstone called the jury practice of convicting of a lesser charge to mitigate against the death penalty as "pious perjury." 4 WILLIAM BLACKSTONE, COMMENTARIES ON THE LAWS OF ENGLAND 239; see also THOMAS ANDREW GREEN, VERDICT ACCORDING TO CONSCIENCE: PERSPECTIVES ON ENGLISH CRIMINAL TRIAL JURY, 1200-1800 295 (1985); LANGBEIN, at 234-35.

[344] There is some disagreement as to how widespread jury sentencing was in non-capital cases at the time of the Constitution's ratification. Compare Adriaan Lanni, Note, Jury Sentencing in Noncapital Cases: An Idea Whose Time Has Come (Again)?, 108 YALE L.J. 1775, 1790 (1999) ("Jury sentencing in noncapital cases was a colonial innovation."), with Nancy J. King & Susan R. Klein, Essential Elements, 54 VAND. L. REV. 1467, 1506 (2001) ("American juries at the time of the adoption of the Bill of Rights played a minor role in sentencing."). Lanni reports that "as recently as three decades ago more than one-quarter of U.S. states provided for jury sentencing in noncapital cases." Lanni, at 1790.

[345] Nancy J. King emphasizes judicial power even in the colonial period through the practice called "benefit of clergy," which derived from seventeenth-century English law. "Clergy was a judicial pardon of sorts," which rested entirely with the judge after conviction. Nancy J. King, "The Origins of Felony Jury Sentencing in the United States, 78 CHI.-KENT L. REV. 938, 948 (2003).

law derived from the common law and in time, statutes from state legislatures—law with which jurors were familiar. [346]

Richard Frase, Excessive Prison Sentences, Punishment Goals, and the Eighth Amendment: "Proportionality" Relative To WHAT? 89 Minn. L. Rev. 571 (2005)

Although the Court has mentioned retributive sentencing goals in numerous Eighth Amendment cases, especially those involving capital punishment, it has never discussed this topic in detail, and has rarely made any reference to the voluminous literature on retributive punishment theory. Several essential points from that literature [347] are relevant here. First, retributive, or "just deserts," theory considers only the defendant's past actions, not his or her probable future conduct or the effects that the punishment might have on crime rates or otherwise. Second, retribution examines the

---

[346] On the absence of federal criminal law, see Sarah Sun Beale, Federalizing Crime: Assessing the Impact on the Federal Courts, 543 ANNALS AM. ACAD. POL. & SOC. SCI. 39, 41 (1996). On the fact that jurors were familiar with the law, see Judith L. Ritter, Your Lips are Moving . . . but the Words Aren't Clear: Dissecting the Presumption that Jurors Understand Instructions, 69 MO. L. REV. 163, 188-189 (2004).

[347] See, e.g., JOSHUA DRESSLER, UNDERSTANDING CRIMINAL LAW 16-18 (3d ed. 2001); JOEL FEINBERG, DOING AND DESERVING: ESSAYS IN THE THEORY OF RESPONSIBILITY (1970); MICHAEL MOORE, PLACING BLAME: A GENERAL THEORY OF THE CRIMINAL LAW (1997); PAUL H. ROBINSON & JOHN M. DARLEY,JUSTICE, LIABILITY, AND BLAME: COMMUNITY VIEWS AND THE CRIMINAL LAW (1995); ANDREW VON HIRSCH, CENSURE AND SANCTIONS (1993).

actor's degree of blameworthiness for his or her past actions, focusing on the offense being sentenced.

Some retributive scholars believe that the current offense is the only relevant consideration and that any prior convictions are irrelevant; other scholars accept that prior crimes modestly increase an offender's blameworthiness. Third, the degree of blameworthiness of an offense is generally assessed according to two kinds of elements: the nature and seriousness of the harm caused or threatened by the crime; and the offender's degree of culpability in committing the crime, in particular, his or her degree of intent (mens rea), motives, role in the offense, and mental illness or other diminished capacity.

Finally, there are two very different theories about the role that retributive values should play in sentencing. These two approaches have sometimes been referred to as "defining" and "limiting" retributivism. [348] According to the first theory, principles of just deserts should define the degree of punishment severity as precisely as possible; offenders should receive their just deserts, no more and no less. This theory, as elaborated by writers such as Andrew von Hirsch, permits crime control, budgetary, or other no retributive values to affect both the overall scale of punishment severity

---

[348] NORVAL MORRIS, MADNESS AND THE CRIMINAL LAW 182-87, 196-202 (1982).

(absolute amounts, as determined by the most and least severe penalties) and the choice among penalties deemed to be equal in severity, but it insists on fairly strict "ordinal" proportionality in the relative severity of penalties imposed on different offenders.

Since defining retributivism leaves little room for the operation of no retributive values and goals, it is clearly too narrow an approach for Eighth Amendment purposes-the Court has made it very clear that states are free to pursue a variety of sentencing goals.

The other theory, limiting retributivism, allows all traditional punishment purposes to play a role but places retributive outer limits both on who may be punished (only those who are blameworthy), and how hard they may be punished (within a range of penalties which would be widely viewed as neither unfairly severe or unduly lenient). This theory, most often associated with the writings of Norval Morris, [349] places particular emphasis on avoiding unfairly

---

[349] Morris's theory is described and critiqued in Richard S. Frase, Limiting Retributivism, in THE FUTURE OF IMPRISONMENT 83 (Michael Tonry ed., 2004) [hereinafter Frase, Limiting Retributivism]. See also Richard S. Frase, Sentencing Principles in Theory and Practice, 22 CRIME & JUST.: REV. RES. 363 (1997) [hereinafter Frase, Sentencing Principles] (comparing Morris's theory to the hybrid approach that has evolved under the Minnesota Sentencing Guidelines Youngjae Lee, The Constitutional Right Against Excessive Punishment, 91 VA L. REV. (forthcoming 2005) (arguing that the Eighth Amendment should recognize retributivism as a "side constraint" on punishment severity). The American Law Institute has recently adopted Morris's limiting retributive theory as the theoretical framework for the revised Model Penal Code sentencing provisions. See MODEL

severe penalties. [350]As revealed in the cases discussed in Part III, limiting retributivism appears to be the approach that the Supreme Court has applied when it has invoked retributive principles. This approach, emphasizing limits on excessive measures, is consistent with both the text of the Eighth Amendment and the role of constitutional guarantees-as protectors of human rights and bulwarks against unfairness and abuse of governmental power.

Proportionality principles are well established in the domestic legal systems of several foreign countries. [351] Perhaps the most well-

---

PENAL CODE § 1.02(2)(a) (Preliminary Draft No. 3, 2004); id. cmt. at 8.

350 K.G. Armstrong writes: Justice gives ... the right to punish offenders up to some limit, but one is not necessarily and invariably obliged to punish to the limit of justice .... For a variety of reasons (amongst them the hope of reforming the criminal) the appropriate authority may choose to punish a man less than it is entitled to, but it is never just to punish a man more than he deserves. K.G. Armstrong, The Retributivist Hits Back, in THE PHILOSOPHY OF PUNISHMENT 138, 155 (H.B. Acton ed., 1969); see also H.L.A. HART, Postscript: Responsibility and Retribution, in PUNISHMENT AND RESPONSIBILITY: ESSAYS IN THE PHILOSOPHY OF LAW 210, 236-37 (1968) ("[M]any self-styled retributivists treat appropriateness to the crime as setting a maximum within which penalties [are chosen on crime-control grounds].("). See generally Frase, Limiting Retributivism, at 92-94 (citing numerous authors and model codes that emphasize strict desert limits on maximum sanction severity, with looser requirements of minimum severity).

351 See, e.g., NICHOLAS EMILLOU THE PRINCIPLE OF PROPORTIONALITY IN EUROPEAN LAW: A COMPARATIVE STUDY 1-3, 23-114 (1996); JURGENSCHWARZE, EUROPEAN ADMINISTRATIVE LAW 680-702 (1992); E. Thomas Sullivan, Antitrust Remedies in the U.S. and EU: Advancing a Standard of Proportionality, 48 ANTITRUST BULL. 377, 415-18 (2003

developed jurisprudence is found in Germany, where three distinct proportionality principles are recognized in administrative and constitutional law: (1) the principle of suitability (public authorities must use means appropriate to the ends they hope to achieve); (2) the principle of necessity (authorities must choose the least harmful, restrictive, or burdensome means available to achieve their ends); and (3) the principle of proportionality in the strict sense (the injury, costs, or burdens of the chosen means must be less than the benefits sought to be gained). The second and third of these principles are clearly recognizable as means and ends proportionality. The first principle is perhaps comparable to the American "rational basis" test, and some writers have argued that it is not really a form of proportionality at all.

Proportionality principles are important not only in German administrative and constitutional law and in sentencing, as discussed above, but also in criminal procedure rules. For example, custodial arrest and pretrial detention are limited by an end's proportionality test; these measures are not permitted if they would be disproportionate to the severity of the offense and the expected penalty. [352] Ends proportionality principles are also implicit in the standards used to determine whether illegally seized evidence can

---

[352] Richard S. Frase & Thomas Weigend, German Criminal Justice as a Guide to American Law Reform: Similar Problems, Better Solutions? 18 B.C. INT'L & COMP. L. REV. 317, 326-28 (1995).

be used at trial. German courts balance the competing interests by weighing the seriousness of the offense, the need for the evidence to support a conviction, and the seriousness of the illegality which led to the evidence. Both ends and means proportionality rules can be found in the laws of many other countries, including Australia, Belgium, Canada, Denmark, England and Wales, France, Ireland, Israel, Italy, Luxembourg, Portugal, South Africa, and Spain.

European Community law now appears to incorporate all three of the German proportionality principles described above, and these principles are also recognized and applied by the European Court of Human Rights. The laws of war, as reflected in The Hague and Geneva Conventions (and before that, religious writings and canon law) also incorporate both ends and means proportionality limitations. Military actions must seek to minimize unnecessary suffering (means proportionality), and must not be excessive relative to the military advantage (ends proportionality) sought to be achieved.

In Ewing, the recent California three strikes case, seven Justices agreed that the Eighth Amendment sets proportionality limits in noncapital cases. However, these Justices disagreed on the application of the proportionality principle in Ewing's case and did not clearly say what they meant by proportionality or how it should apply to non retributive sentencing goals. As shown in this Article, both retributive proportionality and two distinct requirements of utilitarian proportionality are well established in other areas of American constitutional law, and also in foreign and international law. Applying these three principles to the assessment of prison terms under the Eighth Amendment would make such assessments more precise, and would make the Supreme Court's jurisprudence more consistent across fields of law.

The Court's decisions in Harmelin and Ewing might be read as holding that a sentence only violates the Eighth Amendment if it is grossly disproportionate in relation to all sentencing purposes. Even under this interpretation, the utilitarian ends and means proportionality principles identified in this Article should still apply disjunctively-only one of them need be violated-because each represents a distinct and important form of utilitarian excess. The better approach would be to apply all three proportionality principles disjunctively, finding an Eighth Amendment violation if any one of the three is violated. The three principles are logically independent, represent distinct values, and operate independently in many other areas of constitutional law.

Independent application of the three proportionality principles is particularly appropriate in making the "threshold" determination of gross disproportionality required under the Court's current Eighth Amendment approach (comparing the gravity of the defendant's offense and the harshness of the penalty, the first Solem factor).

Without further modification, the standards guiding this threshold determination are extremely vague, and the language and results in Harmelin and Ewing suggest that virtually no cases will survive that determination. Applying the three proportionality principles would add greater precision and some degree of objectivity to the threshold standard. Applying these principles independently would allow additional cases to become eligible for intra- and inter-jurisdictional comparisons under the more objective second and third Solem factors. It is particularly important to recognize retributive proportionality limits316 on lengthy prison terms under the Eighth Amendment. Punishment in excess of blameworthiness is fundamentally unfair and a violation of human rights. Limiting retributivism is a sound jurisprudential principle which enjoys widespread support, and the Supreme Court has used this principle to place constitutional limits on the imposition of capital punishment, fines and forfeitures, and punitive damages. As the latter examples show, even serious wrongdoers are entitled to proportionate punishment. Prison terms may be less severe and final than capital punishment, but they are often far more onerous for the individual than fines, forfeitures, and punitive damages; there is no good reason to set retributive upper limits on the latter, but not on lengthy prison terms. Appellate courts and articles such as this one necessarily deals in abstractions-legal principles, applied within and across factual contexts.

But it is important for courts and scholars to keep in mind the human reality of the specific context at issue-in this case, the reality of what a lengthy prison term means for the offender and his family. Foremost, of course is the loss of freedom -decades of a person's life, caged like an animal, usually the best years, and often most of the person's remaining years. Long prison terms also impose extended or even permanent loss of social status and employability; lost privacy and dignity; substantial risk of serious physical injury from more or less forcible rape, other assaults, HIV, and other infections; constant fear of these assaults and injuries; and as the ultimate result, profound demoralization, dehumanization, and brutalization.322 Of course, the things that criminals do to their victims, the harms they cause and the fears they stir up, are also very serious. But as indicated by the six modern cases in the Supreme Court, most Eighth Amendment proportionality cases are not about violent offenders, or even high-level drug dealers. They are mostly about repeat property offenders, most of whom have serious drug or alcohol dependencies and/or mental health problems-people who are basically just a nuisance, who we wish would go away.

Violations of utilitarian proportionality also have important constitutional implications whenever the accused citizen's physical liberty, security, or other fundamental rights are threatened. Utilitarian ends and means proportionality principles are well established in many areas of American constitutional law. In sentencing, as in these other areas, government measures may be found unconstitutional if they are excessively intrusive relative to their supposed benefits, and/or if they are much more intrusive than equally effective, alternative measures. The Supreme Court is understandably reluctant to give broad effect to any of these proportionality principles under the Eighth Amendment, for reasons of federalism and democratic legitimacy-state legislators, chief executives, prosecutors, and offender is likely to face, and any physical or other vulnerabilities that would make the prison sentence particularly severe for the offender.

MEANINGFUL PROPORTIONALITY REVIEW OF SENTENCES MUST BE MANDATORY IN ARIZONA BY STATE AND FEDERAL JUDGES. THE EXCESSIVE DEFERENCE TO LEGISLATURES WHO ENACTED VINDICTIVE PENALTIES VIOLATES THE CRUEL AND UNUSUAL PROVISION AND ICCPR

James J. Brennan, The Supreme Court's Excessive Deference to Legislative Bodies under Eighth Amendment Sentencing Review, 94 J.Crim. L. & Criminology 551 (2003-2004)

In Ewing v. California, [353] five Justices of the Supreme Court held that the Eighth Amendment does not prohibit the State of California from sentencing a repeat felon[354] to life imprisonment without the possibility of parole for the first twenty-five years of the term for the theft of $1,200 worth of golf clubs under the State's "Three Strikes and You're Out Laws." [355] Nonetheless, seven Justices restated that the Eighth Amendment forbids prison sentences that are grossly

---

[353] 538 U.S. 11, 30-31 (2003) (plurality opinion).

[354] Id. (plurality opinion); id. at 32 (Scalia, J., concurring in the judgment); id. (Thomas, J., concurring in the judgment).

[355] Id. at 23 (plurality opinion); id. at 35 (Breyer, J.,di ssenting).

disproportionate to the crime. The Court's plurality opinion applied the analytical framework introduced in Justice Kennedy's concurring opinion in Harmelin v. Michigan, [356] which counsels judges to consider four principles when assessing disproportionate sentencing claims. First, criminal punishment determinations are normally the province of legislative bodies. Second, the Eighth Amendment allows a variety of legitimate penological theories beyond retribution.' Third, the nature of our federal system allows diverse sentencing determinations among the States! Finally, proportionality review should be guided by objective factors. The Court held that California's policy decision to incapacitate criminals who have already been convicted of at least one serious or violent crime was constitutional.' [357]

This Note argues that the Supreme Court's decision was wrong because it gives too much deference to legislative bodies. The Court needs to assert a more active role in protecting an individual's Eighth Amendment protection from excessive prison sentence. In addition, the Court needs to define the elements it considers under prison sentence review. This Note examines: (1) the legal history and Supreme Court case law on the issue of proportionality in criminal sentencing; (2) the background and procedural history of Ewing's

---

[356] 501 U.S. 957, 998-1001 (1991) (Kennedy, J., concurring in part and concurring in the judgment).
[357] 538 U.S. at 31 (plurality opinion).

disproportionate sentencing claim; (3) the positions taken by the Justices in their final determination of the case; (4)the effect the Court's decision will have on sentence proportionality claims; and (5) the Court's sentence proportionality jurisprudence.

The Ewing Court held that the Eighth Amendment's proportionality requirement did not prohibit the State of California from sentencing a repeat felon to a prison term of twenty-five years to life under the State's "Three Strikes and You're Out Laws." A majority of the Court correctly affirmed that the Eighth Amendment has a proportionality principle that applies to noncapital sentences. But the Court's opinion gives too much deference to legislative bodies and not enough consideration to an individual's constitutional right to protection from excessive punishment.

Julian C. Jr. D'Esposito, Sentencing Disparity: Causes and Cures, 60 J. Crim. L. Criminology & Police Sci. 182 (1969)

Sentencing theories have fluctuated between two extremes: identical disposition of all persons convicted of the same offense, [358] and individualized disposition based on the character of the offender.

---

[358] C. BECCARIA, AN ESSAY ON CRIMES AND PUNISHMENTS (2d ed. English trans. 1769).

The rigidity and consequent harshness of uniform sentencing [359] applied without reference to aggravating or mitigating factors led to the development of the indeterminate sentence, parole, and other forms which took into account the personality of the offender and the circumstances of the offense. Individualized disposition as it exists today, however, presents the possibility that the judge will abuse his discretion by imposing different sentences for the same offense without justification., Since the purpose of individualized sentencing is to base the punishment on the personality of the criminal [360] as well as the gravity of the crime, statistics should show differences in sentence for the same crime. Disparity, however, is unjustified if the rationale for these differences cannot be traced to relevant distinctions of character or behavior which bear a certain known relationship to the aims of punishment. Individualized sentencing is abused when the type and length of sentence depends on the identity of the particular trial judge exercising unchecked judicial discretion within a wide range of statutory sentencing alternatives.

In the United States the trial judge has no external legislative guidelines which delineate sentencing factors and their relative weight. Although most judges could point to factors which influence

---

[359] P. TAPPAN, CRIME, JUSTICE AND) CORRECTION 430-31 (1960).

[360] George, Comparative Sentencing Techniques, 23 FED. PROB. 27 (1959).

their choice of sentence, these factors lack objectivity. In another courtroom the same factors might be ignored or given different weight in the imposition of sentence. Subjectivity in sentencing, lack of proper guidelines, and virtual absence of limitations on the exercise of judicial discretion have produced unjustified disparity.

To individualize sentences properly the judge must first differentiate between the offender and others with regard to personality, character, socio-cultural background, the motivations of his crime, and his particular potentialities for reform or recidivism. Then he must determine which among a range of punitive, corrective, psychiatric, and social measures is best adapted to solve the individualized set of problems presented by that offender so his propensity for recidivist conduct is reduced.[361]

The imposition of disparate sentences upon offenders with similar characteristics convicted of similar crimes hinders correctional methods. When an offender receives an unjustified sentence, his antagonism toward society is increased. He becomes a discipline problem, and a barrier to rehabilitation is erected. His family lives in an aura of injustice. Confidence in the administration of the legal system is shaken. Not only does disparity harm the prisoner and the prison system, but it is contrary to the basic concept of equal

---

[361] Glueck, The Sentencing Problem, 20 FED. PROB. 15 (Dec. 1956).

treatment under the law embodied in the Fifth and Fourteenth Amendments to the Constitution." Distinctions in treatment should be neither arbitrary nor unreasonable; they should be based on rational distinctions rooted in significant factual differences which have a substantial relation to a legitimate governmental purpose.

A committee appointed in Connecticut to study the causes of prison unrest and riots noted the relationship between prisoner discontent and alleged inequality in sentences. [362] There is no factor more disturbing to institutional routine and discipline than the question of comparative justice. Prisoners finding themselves convicted of similar crimes, compare experiences and quickly make evaluations which lead to the conclusion that they were unfairly punished. This feeling is frequently found to be the germ of much rioting and disorder and the basis of many serious escapes and other crimes within institutions.[363] Moreover, prisoners leaving our institutions, embittered and laboring under the feeling that they have been mistreated, return to the community and frequently pursue a career of crime with serious results to local communities.[364]

---

[362] Note, Appellate Review of Primary Sentencing Decisions: A Connecticut Case Study, 69 YALE L. J. 1453, 1460 (1960).

[363] Smith, The Sentencing Council and the Problem of Disproportionate Sentences, 11 PRAC. LAW 12, 13 (Feb. 1965).

[364] Flannagan, Reasons for Creation of a Court of Sentence Adjustment (unpublished report), quoted in Ploscowe, The Court and the Correctional System, in CONTEMPORARY CORRECION 57 (P. Tappan ed. 1951).

"Due process is secured by laws operating on all alike, not subjecting the individual to the arbitrary exercise of the powers of government unrestrained by the established principles of private right and distributive justice.[365] Laws may not be unreasonable, arbitrary, or capricious. The means chosen by the government must have a substantial relation to the object sought to be obtained.[366]

Traditional notions of due process and equal protection must provide the legal framework for the development of individualized treatment of offenders based on the type of offense, the personality of the offender, and individual and societal needs for deterrence. Where the inadequacy of institutional resources and insufficient knowledge about correctional goals and methods enlarge the difficulties of properly individualized sentencing, the type and length of penal disposition should be closely balanced by social and legal notions of equality. Legal structures make their singular contribution to the dilemma of the trial judge who must make and act on judgments where a lack of certainty about dispositional effectiveness makes the reliability and validity of such judgments questionable. The existing system, although it offers a reasonable and desirable opportunity for individualized sentencing, jails to provide adequate standards for sentencing and sufficient checks

---

365 Caldwell v. Texas, 137 U.S. 692 (1891).
366 Nebbia v. New York, 291 U.S. 502 (1933). " But see Lewis, The Humanitarian Theory of Punishment, 6 RES JUDICATE 224 (1953).

upon the exercise of judicial discretion. It is this failure that has produced unjustified and harmful sentence disparity in the United States.

The trend toward individualized disposition has produced widespread differences in sentences imposed upon offenders convicted of the same crime. Some of these differences are attributable to valid objective factors. But in other cases, the disparity can only be attributed to the identity of the trial judge and cannot be rationally justified. Subjective and ambiguous perception of the relevant factors in sentencing by the trial bench has produced unjustified disparity in sentences.

Until sentencing factors become more capable of objective determination, the legal system should provide boundaries for the exercise of judicial discretion. The sentencing function should be left to the unchecked discretion of the trial judge only when the exercise of that discretion becomes totally just and scientific. Pending a more adequate formulation of sentencing objectives and factors, the sentencing process should be reformed by revision of penal codes to control the use of the indeterminate sentence and to distinguish between the ordinary and extended sentence, and by appellate review of sentences.

Paul J. Sullivan, Sentencing: Disparity, Inconsistency, and a New Federal Criminal Code, 20 Cath. U. L. Rev. 748 (1971).

Inconsistency in penalty provisions has been one of the foremost problems of our sentencing system. For example, a person convicted of making a "false, fictitious, or fraudulent" claim against a government department or agency subjects himself to five years imprisonment and a $10,000 fine, while a person convicted of a similar false claim in excess of $100 against the Post Office Department is subjected only to one year imprisonment and a $500 fine." The existence of this disparity leads arguably to unequal treatment of some criminals. Prison discipline likewise is affected when inmates discover that their sentences are harsher than those of prisoners convicted of more serious offenses. The principal factor leading to inconsistent penalty provisions is the "piecemeal" approach to the treatment of criminal issues. Title 18, like most state penal codes, was enacted on a "piecemeal" basis by "numerous differently composed legislatures'" [367] with their own view as to what sentence best fits the crime. Professor Herbert Wechsler has bitterly criticized this "piecemeal" approach.

No branch of penal legislation is, in my view, more unprincipled or more anarchical than that which deals with prison terms that may or

---

[367] Note, Statutory Structures for Sentencing Felons to Prison, 60 COLUM. L. RE V. 1134, 1138 (1960).

sometimes must be imposed on conviction of specific crimes. The legislature typically makes determinations of this order not on any systematic basis but rather by according its ad hoc attention to some discrete area of criminality in which there is a current hue and cry. Distinctions are thus drawn which do not have the slightest bearing on the relative harmfulness of conduct and the consequent importance of preventing it so far as possible, on the probable dangerousness of the individual whose conduct is involved, or even on a public demand for heavy sanctions which is so inexorable that it cannot safely be denied. What dictates legislation is the simple point of politics that reelection demands voting against sin, whenever ballots on the question must be cast. Congressman Celler has voiced a similar but more reserved criticism: The penalties imposed at other times and places have reflected the cultural preferences and exigencies of the era rather than any real attempt to weigh the value of the methods in use. [368]

It appears that a primary cause of sentence inconsistency is the enactment of criminal statutes with little consideration of what sentences are currently authorized for equally grave crimes.' Thus, a congressional committee considering what maximum sentence to fix for robbery of a post office, for example, should consider initially the present penalty for robbery of other federal buildings. As a result

---

[368] Pilot Institute on Sentencing, 26 F.R.D. 231, 243 (1960) (remarks of Rep.Celler).

of this "piecemeal" approach, there are a large and irrational number of federal sentencing categories. Title 18 contains some 55 distinct punishment categories. Among these categories are 18 separate and distinct maximum prison terms ranging from 30 days to life imprisonment and death,' 14 different fine levels ranging from $50 to $25,000, and various combinations of other prison terms and fines. Such numerous sentencing distinctions are clearly "in excess of those which could rationally be drawn on the basis of relative harmfulness of conduct or the probable dangerousness of the offenders. [369]Consequently, the Commission has recommended that Congress place criminal sentences within a few broad categories relating to the seriousness of the crime.[370]

The present federal criminal code is grossly inadequate. It is not structured rationally, and is little more than a poorly organized compilation of existing criminal statutes. The most promising aspect of the Commission's proposed code is the attempt to integrate the various code sections into a rational scheme. [371]This is particularly

---

369 THE PRESIDENT'S COMMISSION OF LAW ENFORCEMENT AND ADMINISTRATION OF JUSTICE, TASK FORCE REPORT: THE COURTS 15 (1967), [hereinafter cited as TASKFORCE REPORT: THE COURTS].

370 PROPOSED NEW FEDERAL CRIMINAL CODE § 3002.

371 The Commission has borrowed substantially from other modem penal codes. See, e.g., ADVISORY COUNCIL OF JUDGES OF THE NATIONAL COUNCIL ON CRIME AND DELINQUENCY, MODEL SENTENCING ACT (1963); AMERICAN LAW INSTITUTE, MODEL PENAL CODE (P.O.D. 1962); AMERICAN BAR

important from the standpoint of sentencing because a criminal offense considered serious enough by Congress to rate a Class A or B felony designation, would automatically authorize the imposition of a Class A or B felony sentence. To this extent, sentences under the proposed code would be more consistent than sentences under current methods. But as noted earlier, mores change and if the new code is to maximize consistency in sentencing, the National Commission on Reform of Federal Criminal Laws should become a permanent body whose function would be to review the code periodically and make recommendations to Congress for its modernization. Without such a body, or other provision for modernization, the new code would once again become stagnant and inconsistent. Under the Commission's proposed code, there would probably be some lessening of disparity in sentencing. In part, this would be accomplished by directing the attention of a judge to "those factors which the legislature had determined to be relevant to the sentencing decision. It appears that the only other successful method within the proposed code for promoting parity in sentencing is the curtailment of long sentences which necessarily leads to a greater limitation of the trial judge's discretion. This is of limited value, however, due to the Commission's recommendation for curtailment of minimum sentences.

ASSOCIATION, STANDARDS RELATING TO SENTENCING ALTERNATIVES AND PROCEDURES (Approved Draft, 1968).

Nancy Keir, Solem v. Helm: Extending Judicial Review under the Cruel and Unusual Punishments Clause to Require "Proportionality" of Prison Sentences, 33 Cath. U. L. Rev. 479 (1984).

Because the language of the eighth amendment is derived from the English Bill of Rights of 1689, the amendment is presumed to afford the individual at least those protections embodied in its English counterpart. It is widely believed that at the time of its adoption the framers of the United States Constitution intended primarily to prohibit punishments that were cruel in their method, rather than excessive in relation to the crime. American courts virtually ignored the cruel and unusual punishments clause for nearly 100 years. United States v. Weems [372] was the first United States Supreme Court decision to articulate the notion that the eighth amendment required a penalty to be in proportion to the crime for which it was imposed.

Until the Supreme Court decided Solem v. Helm, the Court had never expressly determined whether the eighth amendment's prohibitions extended to sentences of imprisonment excessive in duration. The holding in Helm extended proportionality concepts expressly to life imprisonment without parole and impliedly to excessive prison sentences. The history of the Supreme Court's treatment of the eighth amendment's "cruel and unusual

---

372 217 U.S. 349 (1910).

punishments" clause permits the Helm Court's conclusion that punishment should be proportionate to the offense committed, regardless of the mode of punishment. The decision is firmly rooted in equitable considerations. Helm cannot, however, rationally be reconciled with the Supreme Court's three-year old Rummel decision. As lower courts are faced with future challenges to prison sentences, they will be forced to consider both Rummel and Helm and attempt to determine the boundary between the two.

Additionally, practical problems may arise in making the necessary factual determinations under Helm: "drawing the line" between constitutionally permissible sentences and those that violate the cruel and unusual punishments clause. It is uncertain after Helm whether life imprisonment for a third, fourth, seventh, or tenth nonviolent felony violates the eighth amendment. Moreover, while life imprisonment imposed for overtime parking would clearly be cruel and unusual, sentences imposed for other types of offenses may be more difficult to evaluate. It will be the close cases that require the in-depth analysis of courts, not the cases that clearly fall within conventional experience. Courts have exhibited competence, however, at making such difficult factual determinations. The proportionality test articulated in Helm will assist courts in making more objective, less arbitrary, determinations under the eighth amendment and will serve to promote the equitable concerns that prompted the amendment's passage.

Allyn G. Heald, CRIMINAL LAW: United States v. Gonzales: In Search of a Meaningful Proportionality Principle, 58 BROOK. L. Rev. 455 (1992).

Those who have challenged their sentences as unconstitutionally disproportionate relied on the Eighth Amendment's Cruel and Unusual Punishments Clause [373] for a guarantee of proportionate sentencing. Although on its face this clause does not guarantee that sentences be proportioned to the offenses committed, English history provides some support for finding such a guarantee. Accordingly, the Supreme Court has recognized, at various times and to various degrees, an Eighth Amendment right to proportionate sentencing.' There is a lively and inconclusive debate over the origins and meaning of the Cruel and Unusual Punishments Clause. Tracing the text of the clause back to the English Declaration of Rights of 1689, historians have been unable to conclude whether the English intended to prohibit only cruel and unusual methods of punishment or whether the clause was aimed at disproportionate punishments as well. [374]

---

373 U.S. CONST. amend. VIII provides: "Excessive bail shall not be required, nor excessive fines imposed, nor cruel and unusual punishments inflicted."

374 JUSTICE STORY, COMMENTARIES ON THE CONSTITUTION OF THE UNITED STATES 750-51 (DaCapo Press 1970) (1883) (The Eighth Amendment was "adopted, as an admonition to all departments of the national government, to warn them against such violent proceedings, as had taken place in England in the arbitrary reigns of some of the Stuarts ... Enormous fines were . . . sometimes imposed, and cruel and vindictive punishments

For the first hundred years of its existence, the Eighth Amendment received scant attention from the Court, and the prevailing view was that it prohibited only cruel and unusual methods of punishment. [375]

---

inflicted."). Not even the Eighth Amendment ratification debates have yielded much insight into the problem since there was little debate on the amendment. See I Annals of the Cong. 754 (J. Gales, ed. 1789) (complete debate). Nonetheless, the Justices have expressed their views on the matter and bring them to bear in their opinions. See, e.g., Weems v. United States, 217 U.S. 349, 393 (1910)(White, J. dissenting)(the English bill of rights contained no theory of proportional punishment); Solem, 463 U.S. at 286 (1983) (Justice Powell asserts that the Framers of the Eighth Amendment adopted the principle of proportionality that was implicit in the English bill of rights.). Most recently, Justice Scalia, in Harmelin v. Michigan, 111 S. Ct. 2680, 2687 (1991), argued that the English cruel and unusual punishments clause had nothing to do with proportionate sentencing, but was meant to prohibit the illegal exercise of royal power. Contrary to Justice Scalia's somewhat isolated view, this Comment presumes that the Eighth Amendment's Cruel and Unusual Punishments Clause does provide a guarantee against disproportionate punishment Moving from that point, the issue becomes how broad a guarantee the Constitution encompasses and how that guarantee is most effectively implemented by courts.

375 During this period, the Eighth Amendment was largely viewed as a prohibition against torture and inhumane forms of punishment It was thought to be a safeguard against such heinous acts as the English practice of "drawing the condemned man on a cart to the gallows, where he was hanged by the neck, cut down while still alive, disemboweled and his bowels burnt before him, and then beheaded and quartered" and burning female felons at the stake. O'Neil v. Vermont, 144 U.S. 323, 339 (1892). The brief presented by the government in Weems reflected this view, arguing that the Eighth Amendment was concerned only with 'mutilations and degradations." 217 U.S. at 356. The Eighth Amendment was invoked at various times to challenge methods of capital punishment. See Wilkerson v. Utah, 99 U.S. 130 (1878) (capital punishment by firing squad not cruel and unusual given that this was a common mode of execution); In re Kemmler, 136 U.S. 436 (1890) (although not a historical punishment, the New York State

The amendment's protection did not extend to a guarantee of proportionate sentencing. [376] In 1892, in O'Neil v. Vermont, [377] the proportionality element of the Cruel and Unusual Punishments Clause was noticed in a dissenting opinion. While the majority would not entertain O'Neil's claim that his sentence was disproportionate, Justice Field stated that the Eighth Amendment was directed not only against barbarous modes of punishment, such as the rack, the thumbscrews and the iron boot, "but against all

---

legislature concluded that death by electrocution was more humane than death by hanging). In addition, the era was marked by the federal judiciary's reluctance to intrude upon what was believed to be the exclusive realm of state courts. Not until the extension of other federal guarantees to the criminally accused and convicted by the Supreme Court under Chief Justice Earl Warren was the Eighth Amendment expressly held applicable to states in Robinson v. California, 370 U.S. 660 (1962) (invalidating a 90-day prison sentence for the crime of being addicted to narcotics).

376 Although it was not yet considered to be within the purview of the Eighth Amendment, the possibility of a proportionality guarantee was referred to on occasion. For example, in Pervear v. Commonwealth, 72 U.S. (5 Wall.) 475, 480 (1866), the Court stated in dicta that if the Eighth Amendment had applied to state legislation, a $50 fine and a term of three months at hard labor would "not be regarded as excessive, cruel, or unusual" for the crime of maintaining a tenement for the sale of liquors without a license. 72 U.S. at 480. The Supreme Judicial Court of Massachusetts, when reviewing a 25-year sentence imposed under a recidivist statute on a defendant convicted of perjury, obtaining property by false pretenses and forgery, stated it was possible "that imprisonment ... for a long term of years might be so disproportionate to the offense as to constitute cruel and unusual punishment." McDonald v. Commonwealth, 173 Mass. 322, 328-29 (1899), aff'd, 180 U.S. 311 (1901).

377 144 U.S. 323 (1892).

punishments which by their excessive length or severity [we]re greatly disproportioned to the offences charged. [378]

The important function the proportionality principle plays in criminal jurisprudence should give courts reason to pause before stripping the doctrine of its value. It is a precept of fairness and justice that greater crimes should merit harsher penalties than lesser crimes. [379] The notion that punishment should be proportional to the seriousness of the offense is fundamental to maintaining an identity between the criminal law and the public's general sense of morality. In this way, proportionate sentencing serves the purpose of instilling respect for penal law. A penal system that imposes severe punishments for minor crimes runs the risk of being discredited and

---

[378] Id. at 339-40. Even before the proportionality principle was officially recognized, Justice Field was engaging in a comparative analysis to other crimes and sentences. He noted that if O'Neil had been convicted of burglary, highway robbery, manslaughter, forgery or perjury he would have received a lesser punishment. Id. at 339. This demonstrates the tendency to resort to a comparative analysis to make an informed objective decision on the proportionality of a sentence.

[379] Roberts v. Collins, 544 F.2d 168 (4th Cir. 1976) (imposition of greater punishment for lesser included offense than is imposed for the greater offense is unconstitutionally disproportionate). Various criminal codes cite proportionate sentencing as an objective to be achieved. See, e.g., MODEL PENAL CODE § 1.02 (setting forth as goals to differentiate on reasonable grounds between serious and minor offenses and to safeguard offenders against excessive, disproportionate or arbitrary punishment); N.Y. PENAL LAW § 1.05 (McKinney 1988)("To differentiate on reasonable grounds between serious and minor offenses and to prescribe proportionate penalties therefore"); CAL. PENAL CODE § 1170(a)(1)(West 1985 & Supp. 1992)(Punishment is "best served by terms proportionate to the seriousness of the offense.")

ridiculed."'[380] The stringent sentences imposed under the Federal Sentencing Guidelines and similar state statutes for relatively minor drug offenses have led to a public outcry that sentences are too harsh, as evidenced by the formation of such groups as Families Against Mandatory Minimums ("FAMM").[381]

---

[380] 65 H.L.A. Hart expresses the concern that where the legal gradation of crimes diverges from a "commonsense scale of gravity," there is a risk of confusing common morality or bringing the law into contempt. H. L. A. HART, THE CONCEPT OF LAW 7-8 (1961).. Thus, disproportionate sentencing leads people to question their generally held beliefs as to what are serious and what are minor offenses. See also N.H. CONST. of 1784, art. XVII, § 1 ("[W]here the same undistinguishing severity is exacted against all offenses the people are led to forget the real distinction in the crimes themselves, and to commit the most flagrant with as little compunction as they do those of the lightest dye."); A.C. Ewing, A Study of Punishment II: Punishment as Viewed by the Philosopher, 21 CANADIAN B. REV. 102, 115 (1943) ("To punish a lesser crime more severely than a greater would be either to suggest to men's minds that the former was worse when it was not, or, if they could not accept this, to bring the penal law in some degree into discredit or ridicule."). Ewing also suggests that unnecessarily harsh penalties can make the criminal appear to be the victim of cruel laws and thus detract attention from the criminal act and focus attention on the cruelty of the punishment. Id.

[381] See Phil Donahue (NBC television broadcast, Apr. 8, 1992)." See Weems v. United States, 217 U.S. 349, 366-67 (1910) ("Such penalties for such offenses amaze those who have formed their conception of the relation of a state to even its 'offending citizens from the practice of the American commonwealths... In re Lynch, 503 P.2d 921, 923 (Cal. 1972) ("By observing this cautious, often burdensome and sometimes unpopular procedure, the courts can often prevent the will of the majority from unfairly interfering with the rights of individuals who ... may be unable to protect themselves through the political process."); Carmona v. Ward, 436 F. Supp. 1153, 1163 (S.D.N.Y. 1977) (Proportionate sentencing protects individuals from "unduly harsh, oppressive, or arbitrary punishments decreed by a majoritarian political system."), rev'd,

As an element of the Eighth Amendment, the proportionality guarantee also aids in defining the relationship between society and its offending members. The Eighth Amendment demands that states treat convicted individuals "with respect for their intrinsic worth as human beings."" The requirement of proportionate sentencing correspondingly restrains the use of legislative power when it is utilized for extreme utilitarian purposes.

Indeed, the congressional debate surrounding the adoption of the Bill of Rights focused on the question of how much limitation to place on the exercise of legislative power. Some convention participants "felt sure that the spirit of liberty could be trusted, and that its ideas would be represented, not debased, by legislation."382

---

576 F.2d 405 (2d Cir. 1978), cert. denied, 438 U.S. 1091 (1979). " Furman v. Georgia, 408 U.S. 238, 270 (1972) (Brennan, J., concurring). ", Philosopher Jeremy Bentham noted the propensity of those vested with power to disregard the dignity of the individual An error [in imposing too severe a penalty] is that to which legislators and men in general are naturally inclined: antipathy, or want of compassion for individuals who are represented as dangerous and vile, pushes them onward to an undue severity. It is on this side ... that we should take the most precautions. Jeremy Bentham, Principles of Penal Law, in 1 J. BENTHAM 4's WORKS 399 (J.Bowring ed., 1843).

382 Weems, 217 US. at372. Patrick Henry, however, "would take no chances. [His] predominant political impulse was distrust of power, and [he] insisted on constitutional limitations against its abuse." Id. A principal motivation behind the adoption of the Eighth Amendment was the belief "that power might be tempted to cruelty." Id. at 373. See also Bellavia v. Fogg, 613 F.2d 369, 376 (2d Cir. 1979) (Mansfield, J., dissenting) ("the Founding Fathers did not vest our legislators with untrammeled discretion to prescribe punishment"). The critical view expressed by Bentham

As[383] the scope of proportionality review has become more restricted; courts have become more silent about the importance of the guarantee as a check on legislative power [384] By adhering to the overly deferential "shock the conscience" standard of review which weakens the proportionality guarantee.

---

and Henry seems particularly applicable to the contemporary legislative response to the illegal drug trade and drug use. In lieu of more education and drug treatment, legislators are quick to condemn and impose extremely harsh sentences. It is not surprising that many of the most difficult proportionality cases involve drug offenses. Drug offenders routinely invoke the proportionality guarantee as a safeguard against supposed legislative excesses. See, e.g., United States v. Ortiz, 742 F.2d 712 (2d Cir.), cert. denied, 469 U.S. 1075 (1984); People v. Broadie, 37 N.Y.2d 100, 332 N.E.2d 338, 371 N.Y.S.2d 471 (1975); Carmona v. Ward, 576 F.2d 405 (2d Cir. 1978), cert. denied, 438 U.S. 1091 (1979); Bellavia v. Fogg, 613 F.2d 369 (2d Cir. 1992]

383 In Terrebonne v. Butler, 848 F.2d 500 (5th Cir. 1988), see infra note 109, the Fifth Circuit, unwilling to interfere with the goals of the Louisiana legislature, upheld a sentence of life imprisonment without parole for a 21-year-old drug addict who was a third-time drug offender. With no lack of sympathy, the court stated that "[i]n this instance, the tiger trap has sprung on a sick kitten; and the point that Louisiana doubtless wishes to make by punishing drug dealers in a signal manner finds a pathetic exemplar in the hapless Terrebonne." Id. at 505. Nonetheless, the court could not "[tamper] with Louisiana's attempts to bring its critical narcotics problem under control." Id.

384 Discussions of the importance of proportionality review as a check on legislative power figure prominently in decisions which hold challenged sentences to be unconstitutionally disproportionate. Conversely, such discussions are noticeably lacking in decisions which have curbed the scope of the review. See, eg., Rummel v. Estelle, 445 U.S. 263 (1980); Harmelin v. Michigan, 111 S. Ct. 2680 (1991).

EFFECTIVE APPLICATION OF CRUEL AND UNUSUAL PUNISHMENT IN ARIZONA MANDATES ALL SENTENCES BE REVISITED BY FEDERAL AND STATE COURTS

Louise S. McAlpin Harmelin v. Michigan: Effective Application of Anti-Drug Legislation or Cruel and Unusual Punishment? Nova Law Review Volume 16, Issue 3 1992 Article 14

The traditional American concept of criminal sentencing is that prisons exist for rehabilitation and release as much as for incarceration. [385] However, in recent years Congress and state legislatures have enacted a series of stringent anti-drug laws, which have largely abandoned the concept of rehabilitating prisoners [386] and instead, focused on keeping inmates locked up for longer periods of time. [387]

---

[385] Michael A. Kroll, The Prison Experiment: A Circular History, S. Exposure,
Winter 1978, at 6. See generally Kurt Anderson, What Are Prisons For?, TIME, Sept. 13, 1982, at 38.

[386] Michael Isikoff and Tracy Thompson, Getting Too Tough on Drugs; Draconian Sentences Hurt Small Offenders More Than Kingpins, THE WASHINGTON POST, November 4, 1990, at Cl.

[387] Brief for Respondent at 2, Harmelin v. Michigan, Ill S. Ct. 2680 (1991) (No. 89-7272) [hereinafter Brief for Respondent].

Since the complete revision of the federal sentencing system in 1984, sentences are no longer rehabilitative in nature and Legislatures are reacting to an ever-increasing spiral of drug traffic, drug abuse and drug-related crime [388] by instituting these harsh penalties in an attempt to thwart drug activity. The result of this "war on-drugs legislation" is an overwhelmed court system and staggering increases in the nation's prison population. Since 1986, average jail time served in federal drug cases is fifty-eight months, an increase of 151 percent. [389] One weapon used in this war-on-drugs is the mandatory life sentence without opportunity of parole, commonly called "life without parole". [390] A mandatory life sentence without parole is the "penultimate penalty", meaning a convict will spend the rest of his natural life behind bars. The recent development and current prevalence of life without parole is due to the fact that it addresses legislative policies underlying criminal

---

[388] Ruth Marcus, Life in Prison For Cocaine Possession? High Court Weighing Strict Michigan Law, THE WASHINGTON POST, November 5, 1990, at A1. Fifty seven percent of a national sample of males arrested in 1989 for homicide tested positive for illegal drugs. National Institute of Justice, 1989 Drug Use Forecasting Annual Report June, 1990. The comparable statistics for assault, robbery and weapons arrests were 55, 73, and 63 percent, respectively. Id. In Michigan, in 1988, 68 percent of a sample of male arrestees and 81 percent of a sample of female arrestees tested positive for illegal drugs. Harmelin v. Michigan, 111 S. Ct. 2680, 2706 (1991) (Kennedy, J., concurring).

[389] Dennis Cauchon, The Scales of Justice May be Tipped Unfairly, USA To-DAY, June 24, 1991, at A8.

[390] Wright, Life-Without-Parole: An Alternative To Death Or Not Much Of A Life At All?, 43 VAND. L. REV. 529 (1990).

penalties. [391] Legislators mandate these life sentences without parole hoping the penalty will not only prevent the offender from injuring others, but also act as a societal deterrent."

Unfortunately these "life without parole sentences" without parole do not produce the desired results and often lead to injustice. Perhaps the most persuasive argument against mandatory life sentences is one of fairness.' [392]While many Americans were unhappy with lenient parole has been eliminated in favor of determinate sentences.

No longer would the judge's discretion be the sole determinate of a criminal's punishment. Rather each drug offender would receive a harsh, but equal treatment. On the contrary, mandatory life sentences have failed to treat all criminals the same. [393]One reason for this inequity is due to the prosecutors' authority to dictate a criminal's penalty by their choice of charges filed. In Harmelin's case, for instance, had prosecutors filed charges against him in federal court, rather than in state court, he would be facing a much

---

[391] See People v. Lemble, 303 N.W.2d 191 (Mich. Ct. App. 1981).

[392] Concerned that mandatory minimum sentences, which already affect about one-third of federal sentences are unfair, judges in several federal circuits have joined in formal protests against this type of sentencing. See Sturgess, Mandatory Sentences Draw Increased Fire; Judges, Families Join Fight Against Minimum Guidelines, THE RECORDER, May 7, 1991 at 1.

[393] W. John Moore, Mindless Minimums, NATIONAL JOURNAL, June I, 1991 at 1310.

more lenient sentence. Another inequity in this anti-drug legislation is the frequency by which large-scale drug traffickers evade these mandatory sentences. It is ironic that drug kingpins, the targets of these anti-drug laws, have been given lesser sentences for providing law enforcement with information regarding their drug ring." In 1988, the House Judiciary Subcommittee on Crime learned of a drug kingpin who was released from custody for providing law enforcement with the names of twelve lower level dealers. All twelve lower-level dealers received mandatory sentences.

In Harmelin v. Michigan, [394] the Supreme Court considered the scope of the Eighth Amendment's prohibition on cruel and unusual punishments against the imposition of a mandatory life sentence without parole for a nonviolent first offense of possession of 672 grams of cocaine. The Court held that "mandatory [life] penalties may be cruel, but they are not unusual in the constitutional sense.'" Accordingly, this decision sharply limits the holding in Solem v. Helm, [395] a 1983 Supreme Court case which incorporated the notion that criminal sentences should be proportional to the crime.

---

394 111 S. Ct. 2680 (1991).
395 463 U.S. 277 (1983)(holding the defendant's sentence was significantly disproportionate to the crime, and therefore was prohibited by the Eight Amendment).

Traditionally, the Eighth Amendment" [396] has regulated the mode of punishment, as well as the length of a sentence. [397] This Comment explores whether the Eighth Amendment's prohibition of cruel and unusual punishments limits the authority of legislatures to prescribe these mandatory life sentences without the possibility for parole. The answer to this issue has both social and legal impacts. As a matter of social policy, this issue poses questions about the purpose of our prison system, the role, if any, of rehabilitation and the degree to which individual moral culpability and mitigating circumstances should be taken into account during sentencing. As a question of law, this issue sheds light on the scope of cruel and unusual punishments under the eighth amendment and the meaning of the proportionality principle as defined in Solem.

This Comment's central thesis is that Harmelin was wrongly decided for three reasons: 1) prior Supreme Court precedent firmly establishes that the power of legislatures to set criminal sentences is subject to an Eighth Amendment proportionality review; 2) mandatory life sentences without parole should be subject to the individualized sentencing prevalent in capital cases, [398] and 3)

---

[396] U.S. CONST. amend. VIII provides that "[e]xcessive bail shall not be required, nor excessive fines imposed, nor cruel and unusual punishments inflicted."

[397] Solem, 463 U.S. at 284.

[398] See, e.g., Gregg v. Georgia, 428 U.S. 153 (1976) (death penalty does not violate Eighth Amendment's ban on cruel and unusual punishment); Woodson v. North California, 428 U.S. 280 (1976);

Harmelin's sentence of life in prison without parole was disproportionate to the crime." This Comment will be divided into five sections. Following this introduction, section II provides an historical analysis of eighth amendment jurisprudence. Specifically, this section interprets the eighth amendment as incorporating a principle of proportionality of punishments. It then examines the evolution of the individualized sentencing doctrine adopted in capital cases. Next, section III reviews the Supreme Court's recent decision in Harmelin v. Michigan. [399]Section IV addresses the flaws in the Michigan statute under which Harmelin received life in prison without parole, and applies the Solem proportionality factors [400] to the facts in Harmelin to demonstrate how the case was wrongly decided. Finally, Section V concludes by stressing the detrimental effects caused by the recent trend of mandatory minimum sentences in anti-drug legislation illustrated by the Michigan statute [401]which was upheld in Harmelin.

The Supreme Court's decision in Harmelin profoundly displays the new boldness of a solidly conservative court which seems determined to subvert individual rights. [402]The Justices' concern

---

Proffitt v. Florida, 428 U.S. 242 (1976); Jurek v. Texas, 428 U.S. 262 (1976).
399 111 S. Ct. 2680 (1991).
400 Solem v. Helm, 463 U.S. 277, 290-93 (1983).
401 MICH. COMP LAWS ANN. § 333.7403 (West 1980).
402 Savage, Justices Uphold Victims' Rights, 'Cruel' Penalties, THE Los ANGELES TIMES, June 28, 1991, § A at 1

over the threat of drugs in society influenced them to uphold a Michigan law imposing a mandatory sentence of life imprisonment without parole for possession of more than 650 grams of cocaine. [403] Consequently, by upholding such an excessive sentence the Court has likened drug possession as the moral equivalent of first-degree murder. Although stiff anti-drug laws have emotional appeal, they frequently do not produce the results expected by legislators, practically speaking, harsh sentences for drug offenses send some non-violent drug dealers to prison for longer terms than murderers, rapists and armed robbers. Therefore, if the eighth amendment's prohibition on cruel and unusual punishment is to retain any vitality, such grossly disproportionate treatment must be outlawed.

Unfortunately, the majority in Harmelin largely abandoned the ancient notion that the punishment must fit the crime. In doing so, the Court sharply limited the Eighth Amendment's prohibition on cruel and unusual punishments. Thus, the Court incorrectly gave a constitutional stamp of approval to the increasingly popular tactic of imposing mandatory minimum terms of imprisonment for drug offenses without consideration of mitigating circumstances or judicial discretion.

---

403 Marcus, High Court Upholds Life Sentence in Drug Case; Mandatory Michigan Penalty Imposed for Possession of 1 Pounds of Cocaine, THE WASHINGTON POST, June 28, 1991, § A at 16.

VINDICTIVE PUNISHMENT IS THE ARIZONA NORM MANDATING REVIEW

Jalila Jefferson-Bullock How Much Punishment Is Enough?: Embracing Uncertainty in Modern Sentencing Reform Journal of Law and Policy http://brooklynworks.brooklaw.edu/jlp Part of the Criminal Law Commons, Criminal Procedure Commons, Law Enforcement and Corrections Commons, Legislation Commons, and the Public Law and Legal Theory Commons

It has now become fashionable to loudly proclaim that the U.S. criminal justice system is irreparably broken and requires a complete dismantling and total reconfiguration. [404] The evidence is

---

[404] See generally Peter Baker, 2016 Candidates are United in Call to Alter Justice System, N.Y. TIMES (Apr. 27, 2015), http://nyti.ms/1DERGad; Peter Baker, Bill Clinton Concedes His Crime Law Jailed Too Many for Too Long, N.Y. TIMES (July 15, 2015), http://nyti.ms/1HvZBL9; Erik Eckholm, A.C.L.U. in $50 Million Push to Reduce Jail Sentences, N.Y. TIMES (Nov. 6, 2014), http://nyti.ms/1uDzbmQ; Bill Keller, Prison Revolt, NEW YORKER (June 29, 2015),
http://www.newyorker.com/magazine/2015/06/29/prison-revolt; Editorial Board, Justice Kennedy's Plea to Congress, N.Y. TIMES (Apr. 4, 2015), http://nyti.ms/1EXdUcJ; Editorial Board, Ending the Rikers Nightmare, N.Y. TIMES (June 24, 2015), http://nyti.ms/1SJ6cH2.

robust and the record is clear. [405]Prisons are bloated and bursting with prisoners; budgets are ill endowed to support them; and offenders, due to excessive periods of unfruitful incapacitation, reenter society lacking in contributable and marketable skills. [406] Racial disparities continue to corrupt charging and sentencing decisions; police brutality and human massacre are, woefully, commonplace; and the cycle continues. [407]

The United States' criminal sentencing laws too often fail to advance any legitimate law enforcement objective. [408]

---

[405] See, e.g., Erik Eckholm, How to Cut the Prison Population (See for Yourself), N.Y. TIMES (Aug. 11, 2015), http://nyti.ms/1L3HwZ4; Ian Lovett, Los Angeles Agrees to Overhaul Jails to Care for Mentally Ill and Curb Abuse, N.Y. TIMES (Aug. 5, 2015), http://nyti.ms/1ORJART; Marc Mauer & David Cole, How to Lockup Fewer People, N.Y. TIMES (May 24, 2015), http://nyti.ms/1dr0RoH.

[406] Jesselyn McCurdy, New Report Shines a Light on Solitary Confinement, AM. CIV. LIBERTIES UNION (June 5, 2013, 11:20 AM), https://www.aclu.org/blog/new-report-shines-light-solitary-confinement; Erica Goode, Solitary Confinement: Punished for Life, N.Y. TIMES (Aug. 3, 2015), http://nyti.ms/1IkH1E3.

[407] John Eligon & Mitch Smith, Emergency Declared in Ferguson After Shooting, N.Y. TIMES (Aug. 10, 2015), http://nyti.ms/1IDHpOa; Adam Liptak, Exclusion of Blacks From Juries Raises Renewed Scrutiny, N.Y. TIMES (Aug. 16, 2015), http://nyti.ms/1LeZEzd; John Eligon, A Year After Ferguson, Housing Segregation Defies Tools to Erase It, N.Y. TIMES (Aug. 8, 2015), http://nyti.ms/1KZj0Z5.

[408] See Jelani Jefferson Exum, Sentencing, Drugs, and Prisons: A Lesson from Ohio, 42 U. TOL. L. REV. 881, 882 (2011) [hereinafter Exum, Sentencing, Drugs, and Prisons]; see also MICHELLE ALEXANDER, THE NEW JIM CROW: MASS INCARCERATION IN THE AGE OF COLORBLINDNESS 59 (2010)

(stating that the war on drugs targeted mostly low-level street dealers). See generally Kate Stith & Steve Y. Koh, The Politics of Sentencing Reform: The Legislative History of the Federal Sentencing Guidelines, 28 WAKE FOREST L. REV. 223, 227 (1993); Thomas Orsagh & Jong-Rong Chen, The Effect of Time Served on Recidivism: An Interdisciplinary Theory, 4 J.QUANTITATIVECRIMINOLOGY 155 (1988) ("[W]hen prisoners serve longer sentences they are more likely to become institutionalized, lose pro-social contacts in the community, and become removed from legitimate opportunities, all of which promote recidivism."). These sentencing laws not only detrimentally impact the individuals who serve the time in prison, they undermine the communities and families who have loved ones behind bars. See generally SENTENCING PROJECT, INCARCERATED PARENTS AND THEIR CHILDREN: TRENDS 1991-2007 (Feb. 2009), http://www.sentencingproject.org/doc/publications/publications/inc_incarcerated parents.pdf; CHARLENE W. SIMMONS, CALIFORNIA RESEARCH BUREAU, CHILDREN OF INCARCERATED PARENTS (Mar. 2000), http://www.library.ca.gov/crb/00/notes/v7n2.pdf; JEREMY TRAVIS ET AL., URBAN INST., FAMILIES LEFT BEHIND: THE HIDDEN COSTS OF INCARCERATION AND REENTRY (2005), http://www.urban.org/UploadedPDF/310882_families_left_behind.pdf.

Academics continue to document these problems and offer concrete solutions. See, e.g., JULIE SAMUELS ET AL., URBAN INST., STEMMING THE TIDE: STRATEGIES TO REDUCE THE GROWTH AND CUT THE COST OF THE FEDERAL PRISON SYSTEM 1 (2013),http://www.urban.org/UploadedPDF/412932-stemming-the-tide.pdf. Even those charged with enforcing the laws agree the system continues to be broken and in need of reform. See, e.g., Eric Holder, U.S. Attn'y Gen., Remarks at the Annual Meeting of the Am. Bar Ass'n's House of Delegates (Aug. 12, 2013), https://www.justice.gov/opa/speech/attorney-general-eric-holder-delivers-remarks-annualmeeting- American-bar-associations; see also MICHAEL HOROWITZ, U.S. OFFICE OF THE INSPECTOR GENERAL, TOP MANAGEMENT AND PERFORMANCE CHALLENGES FACING THE DEPARTMENT OF JUSTICE (2013), http://www.justice.gov/oig/challenges/2013.htm (listing the "growing crisis in the federal prison system" as a top management

Criminologists, judges, practitioners, political leaders on both sides of the aisle, social scientists, other impartial observers, and even President Obama point to wasted fiscal resources, overcrowded prisons and court dockets, growing recidivism rates, and overly punitive punishment as significant failures that sentencing reform must correct immediately. [409] After decades of imposing an ill-reasoned sentencing regime on multiple generations of offenders, federal sentencing reform is finally upon us. Federal lawmakers are poised to reform criminal sentencing laws now. [410] There are many roots of this criminal justice crisis and numerous injurious fruits

---

and performance challenge); Editorial Board, Prison Reform: Seize the Moment, CHRISTIAN SCI. MONITOR (Aug. 12, 2013), http://www.csmonitor.com/Commentary/the-monitorsview/2013/0812/Prison-reform-Seize-the-moment.

409 In a speech to the American Bar Association, former Attorney General Eric Holder censured the use of excessive prison terms as an unsound criminal justice tool, blaming inflexible mandatory minimum sentences and like practices for unreasonable sentencing disparities, unsustainable prison overcrowding, astronomical recidivism, illogical financial burden, and an overall ineptitude in achieving any true goal of criminal punishment. resident Obama has proclaimed that the time is ripe for sentencing reform.

410 According to President Obama, "We should pass a sentencing reform bill through Congress this year." Concrete efforts have already been made to follow through on this declaration. See, e.g., Corrections Oversight, Recidivism Reduction, and Eliminating Costs for Taxpayers in Our National

System Act, S. 467, 114th Cong. (2015); Smarter Sentencing Act, S. 502, 114th Cong. (2015); Sensenbrenner-Scott SAFE Justice Reinvestment Act of 2015, H.R. 2944, 114th Cong. (2015).

borne of it. [411] Countless well-intended proposals have emerged to cure federal punishment of its ills, [412] yet one simple remedy emerges as a leader in overhauling our outmoded, unjust sentencing structure: abolishing lengthy, determinate federal criminal sentences will cure a litany of America's criminal justice ills. [413] The enactment of lengthy criminal sentence legislation relied on two misguided beliefs: (1) that long sentences can achieve utilitarian and retributive punishment purposes; and (2) that law and policy makers and judges can accurately predict how much punishment is enough at sentencing. [414]In an effort to appear tough on crime, lawmakers chose long sentencing periods almost arbitrarily, with no empirical

---

411 These "fruits" include, but are not limited to, prison overpopulation, recidivism, exorbitant cost, and separation of families. See generally Jalila

Jefferson-Bullock, The Time is Ripe to Include Considerations of the Effects on Families and Communities of Excessively Long Sentences, 83 UMKC L. REV. 73 (2014).

412 S. 467; S. 502; H.R. 2944

413 Marc Santora, City's Annual Cost Per Inmate Is $168,000, Study Finds, N.Y. TIMES (Aug. 23, 2013), http://nyti.ms/17QnidC; Erica Goode, Prisons Rethink Isolation, Saving Money, Lives and Sanity, N.Y. TIMES (Mar. 10, 2012), http://nyti.ms/18RVtb3; Brandi Grissom, Proposals Could Make It Harder to Leave Prison, N.Y. TIMES, (Mar. 12, 2011), http://nyti.ms/1Tz8Lx3; Helen Vera, The Definitive Case for Ending Solitary Confinement, SLATE (Feb. 26, 2014) http://www.slate.com/articles/news_and_politics/jurisprudence/2014/02/against_solitary_confinement_states_are_finding_it_s_impractical_as_well.html.

414 PAUL H. ROBINSON, DISTRIBUTIVE PRINCIPLES OF CRIMINAL LAW: WHO SHOULD BE PUNISHED HOW MUCH? 81 (2008) [hereinafter ROBINSON, DISTRIBUTIVE PRINCIPLES].

foundation or justification for sentence length. [415] It is now painfully obvious that lawmakers indiscriminately created an overly punitive sentencing scheme with disastrous outcomes. [416]Strict, determinate sentencing ignores the indispensable and often overlooked principle of uncertainty. While we know that the current federal sentencing scheme is broken, we are unsure of how to design a new sentencing structure.

The goals of federal punishment, as expressed in 18 U.S.C. § 3553(a), rely on both utilitarian and retributivist principles that profess to punish offenders for both a larger societal benefit and to

---

[415] See, e.g., Michael Isikoff & Tracy Thompson, Getting Too Tough on Drugs: Draconian Sentences Hurt Small Offenders More than Kingpins, WASH.POST (Nov. 4, 1990),
https://www.washingtonpost.com/archive/opinions/1990/11/04/gettingtoo-tough-on-drugs/2b616e5c-e450-47d9-ad6d-09e0c83d449b/; Peter Beinart, Hillary Clinton and the Tragic Politics of Crime, ATLANTIC (May 1, 2015); see also Jeff Stein, The Clinton Dynasty's Horrific Legacy: How "Tough-on-Crime" Politics Built the World's Largest Prison System, SALON (Apr. 13, 2015),
http://www.salon.com/2015/04/13/the_clinton_dynastys_horrific_legacy_how_tough_on_crime_politics_built_the_worlds_largest_prison/; Ben Schreckinger &Annie Karni, Hillary Clinton's Criminal Justice Plan: Reverse Bill's Policies,POLITICO (Apr. 29, 2015), http://www.politico.com/story/2015/04/hillaryclintons-criminal-justice-plan-reverse-bills-policies-117488.

[416] William Spade, Jr., Beyond the 100:1 Ratio: Towards A Rational Cocaine Sentencing Policy, 38 ARIZ. L. REV. 1233, 1266 (1996); Carrie Johnson, 20 Years Later, Parts Of Major Crime Bill Viewed As Terrible Mistake, NPR (Sept. 12,2014),
http://www.npr.org/2014/09/12/347736999/20-years-later-major-crimebill-viewed-as-terrible-mistake.

properly penalize moral blameworthiness. [417] The statute offers deterrence of specific offenders, incapacitation, crime prevention, distribution of just punishment, and effective offender rehabilitation as appropriate sentencing goals. According to 18 U.S.C. § 3553(a), federal criminal punishment must align with the aforementioned objectives, and they should directly inform the length of criminal sentences. Regrettably, our current federal incarceration scheme fails to fully achieve the purposes of 18 U.S.C. § 3553(a) or any other U.S. penal code, and it has become evident that the damage done to society and offenders due to these exorbitantly long sentences is a substantial enough reason to restructure the components of federal sentencing.

As modern-day reformers attempt to reinvent federal sentencing laws, myriad questions must be answered: is incarceration still the preferred punishment method? If so, how long must an offender remain incarcerated? If not, how should offenders be punished? Where should the punishment floor or point of departure begin? And notwithstanding the punishment mode, how much punishment is enough? This article submits that the current sentencing reform debate must embrace the "principle of uncertainty" by admitting the impracticality of determining the appropriate duration of

---

417 See 18 U.S.C. § 3553(a) (2012).

incarceration at sentencing. [418] When attempting to solve a problem involving a high degree of doubt or improbability, the principle of uncertainty acknowledges what we do not yet know, accepts the uncertainty, and then borrows from experimentalist theory to create best practices that will assist in resolving the problem. This principle must be honored in order to properly reapportion federal criminal sentencing laws.

Determinate sentencing was instituted, in part, to remedy the unfairness and lack of uniformity inherent in indeterminate sentencing. [419] In its present form, however, determinate sentencing has proven too rigid and far too excessive. [420] This is its critical

---

[418] The "principle of uncertainty" is a term coined by the author. The concept is borne of experimentalist literature theories.

[419] Modern-day determinate federal sentencing is a product of the Sentencing Commission's work under the Comprehensive Crime Control Act of 1984. U.S. SENT'G COMM'N, AN OVERVIEW OF THE UNITED STATES SENTENCING COMMISSION [hereinafter U.S. SENT'G COMM'N], http://www.ussc.gov/About_the_Commission/Overview_of_the_USSC/USSC_ Overview.pdf (last visited July 12, 2016). Determinate sentences are definite in length and are not reviewed by parole boards. Stanley A. Weigel, The Sentencing Reform Act of 1984: A Practical Appraisal, 36 UCLA L. REV 83, 89–93 (1988).

[420] Press Release, Justice Policy Inst., How To Safely Reduce Prison Population and Support People Returning To Their Communities 1 (June 2, 2010), http://www.justicepolicy.org/images/upload/10-06_fac_forimmediaterelease_psac. pdf ("Contributing to the total number of people incarcerated is the reluctance of parole boards to grant parole to all people who are eligible. Parole boards often face public scrutiny if someone they release commits a new offense.").

defect. Its predecessor, indeterminate sentencing, while flawed in application, [421]was more ideologically sound. Indeterminate sentencing permitted, through federal parole review, evaluations of whether continued incapacitation was necessary post incarceration. [422] Indeterminate sentencing acknowledged that it is impossible to

---

[421] See, e.g., OFFICE OF THE INSPECTOR GEN., U.S. DEP'T OF JUSTICE, THE IMPACT OF ANAGING INMATE POPULATION ON THE FEDERALBUREAU OF PRISONS 3,
https://oig.justice.gov/reports/2015/e1505.pdf ("Research indicates that the growth in the aging inmate population can be attributed to sentencing reforms beginning in the late 1980s, including the elimination of federal parole and the introduction of mandatory minimums and determinate sentences."); Jeremy Ashkenas & Haeyoun Park, The Race Gap in America's Police Departments, N.Y. TIMES (Apr. 8, 2015),
http://nyti.ms/1u2lVGc; Charles M. Blow, Black Lives and Books of the Dead, N.Y. TIMES (July 9, 2015),
http://nyti.ms/1HhEhc9; Jeffery Goldberg, A Matter of Black Lives, ATLANTIC (Sept. 2015)
http://www.theatlantic.com/magazine/archive/2015/09/a-matter-of-lacklives/ 399386/; Nick Pinto, The Bail Trap, N.Y. TIMES MAG. (Aug. 13, 2015), http://nyti.ms/1L82Hcv; Sharon LaFraniere et al., Texas County's Racial Past Is Seen as Prelude to Sandra Bland's Death, N.Y. TIMES (July 26, 2015),
http://nyti.ms/1SJ4hAp; Kevin Sack & Megan Thee-Brenan, Poll Finds Most in U.S. Hold Dim View of Race Relations, N.Y. TIMES (July 23, 2015), http://nyti.ms/1JBB3P4; Brent Staples, Opinion, The Racist Origins of Felon Disenfranchisement, N.Y. TIMES (Nov. 18, 2014), http://nyti.ms/1qnflv5; Seth Stoughton, How Police Training Contributes to Avoidable Deaths, ATLANTIC (Dec. 12, 2014),
http://www.theatlantic.com/national/archive/2014/12/policegun-shooting-training-ferguson/383681/; Justin Wolfers et al., 1.5 Million Missing Black Men, N.Y. TIMES (Apr. 20, 2015),
http://nyti.ms/1P5JAPc.
[422] Weigel, at 104 (noting how the new sentencing guidelines "eliminate[d] the ability of the Parole Commission to respond to prison overcrowding by paroling less dangerous offenders").

accurately determine duration of incapacitation at sentencing. [423]Creation of a new sentencing structure that utilizes a sentencing effectiveness assessment tool post-sentencing will assist lawmakers in formulating rational sentences that appropriately punish offenders and benefit society.

This article proposes an alternative federal sentencing model that embraces the principle of uncertainty. This new model will punish the illegal behavior of offenders, while accepting that, currently, tools do not exist to accurately apportion punishment at sentencing. It will also argue that probation or home incarceration is an appropriate floor or point of departure for most federal offenses. Part I of this article provides lessons learned from the pre-Sentencing Reform Act ("SRA") rehabilitative sentencing model by presenting a glimpse of the history of criminal sentencing in the United States, emphasizing the shift from indeterminate to determinate sentencing. Part II considers the failures wrought by the SRA and questions the logic of that reform. Part III examines current criminal sentencing reform-seeking legislation, assesses the oft neglected principle of uncertainty, and argues for its inclusion in the current sentencing reform debate. Part IV critiques the presumption of prison, examines the impact to offenders and the entire community of lengthy, determinate sentences, and argues that none of these outcomes are

---

423 Indeterminate sentencing consists of a range of years, with a minimum term, but an uncertain release date that is regulated by parole review. Id.

aligned with stated goals of federal sentencing. Finally, Part V offers an alternative model of federal criminal sentencing that both promotes sentencing goals and supports offender and community success by embracing uncertainty. This article does not propose the total abolition of incarceration. [424] Instead, it proposes a new model of sentencing, which ensures that offenders are adequately and fairly punished and prepared to successfully reenter society.

---

[424] This article also does not suggest that particularly heinous crimes do not warrant lengthy prison or other terms of incapacitation.

PORTIONING PUNSHMENT SHOULD BE REQUIRED IN ARIZONA AS THE PUNISHMENT IS CRUEL AND UNUSUAL AND DISPROPORATIONATE UNDER AMERICAN AND INTERNATIONAL STANDARDS

Nancyj. King Portioning Punishment: Constitutional Limits Onsuccessive and Excessive Penalties University of Pennsylvania Law Review [vol. 144:101

There has been a remarkable increase during the last decade in the imposition of overlapping civil, administrative, and criminal sanctions for the same misconduct,' as well as a steady rise in the severity of those sanctions. In response, defendants have balked, Special taxes, forfeitures, and penalties of various kinds are commonly extracted in addition to criminal convictions, , and criminal conduct is punishable under multiple criminal and civil statutes. In several states, for example, a drug offender may face fines, imprisonment, civil forfeiture, and a tax for the same conduct. 425

---

425 see also PETER FINN & MARIA 0. HYLTON, U.S. DEP'T OF JUSTICE, USING CIVIL REMEDIES FOR CRIMINAL BEHAVIOR: RATIONALE, CASE STUDIES, AND CONSTITUTIONAL ISSUES 9-78 (1994) (discussing the use of civil remedies for a variety of

Undoubtedly, the cumulative review of penalties King proposes requiring judges to make difficult distinctions, including when civil sanctions are punishment, which penalties must be considered together, and when combined penalties become unconstitutionally severe. But the difficulties are not insurmountable. Perhaps the best proof of the practicality of this approach is the willingness of judges to adopt it on their own. Several judges have already begun to consider total punishment under the Eighth Amendment regardless of when, where, or how many penalties are imposed. For instance, a panel of the Sixth Circuit recently evaluated a cruel and unusual punishment challenge to consecutive sentences for a firearms

---

criminal behavior, using case studies, and outlining effective and constitutionally defensible ways of using such remedies); Mary M. Cheh, Constitutional Limits on Using Civil Remedies to Achieve Criminal Law Objectives: Understanding and Transcending the Criminal-Civil Law Distinction, 42 HASTINGS LJ. 1325, 1325-27, 1333-44 (1991) (illustrating with examples why "the current phenomenon of civil remedies blending with criminal sanctions never has been more actively or consciously pursued" and surveying how civil remedies are "used to complement enforcement of the criminal law"); PeterJ. Henning, Precedents in a Vacuum: The Supreme Court Continues to Tinker with Double Jeopardy, 31 AM. CRIM. L. REV. 1, 4-5, 34-35 (1993) (describing overlapping penalties). For a thorough and recent analysis of the increased role of punitive civil sanctions in law enforcement, see Kenneth Mann, Punitive Civil Sanctions: The Middle ground Between Criminal and Civil Law, 101 YALE L.J. 1795, 1796-98, 1800-01, 1844, 1849-54 (1992); see also Sandra Guerra, The Myth of Dual Sovereignty: Multijurisdictional Drug Law Enforcement and Double Jeopardy, 73 N.C. L. REV. 1159, 1207-08 & n.245 (1995) (stating that successive prosecutions by state and federal prosecutors, "although still a small fraction of the total volume of criminal cases, have proliferated" and citing examples).

conviction and a robbery conviction arising out of the same conduct by evaluating the total punishment for both penalties together.[426] Other courts evaluating excessive fines challenges to civil forfeitures that follow convictions are asking whether the owner has been "sufficiently punished" for his conduct by the criminal sentence so that further punishment through civil forfeiture would be excessive.[427] Judges considering Paul Robinson and John

---

426 PAUL H. ROBINSON &JOHN M. DARLEYJUSTICE, LIABILITY, AND BLAME: COMMUNITY VIEWS AND THE CRIMINAL LAW 189-97 (1995).

427 See United States v. Duerson, 25 F.3d 376, 384 (6th Cir. 1994) ("Congress contemplated that the penalties for the two rimes ... could reach a total of 360 months, and we are not prepared to say that a total of 157 months is either cruel or unusual." (emphasis added)). See, e.g., United States v. 461 Shelby County Rd. 361, 857 F. Supp. 935, 939-40 (N.D. Ala. 1994) (finding that further punishment of homeowners through forfeiture of their $70,000 home was excessive, considering that the owners, husband and wife, had each pled guilty to drug charges, served their five year sentences (custody and probation, respectively) and had paid or were paying the fines, court costs, and restitution ordered as part of their sentence). Courts considering the excessiveness of criminal forfeiture have also considered related sentences of imprisonment. See, e.g., United States v. Alexander, 32 F.3d 1231, 1237 (8th Cir. 1994) (ordering the district court on remand for excessiveness analysis to "consider the sentences imposed in determining whether the forfeiture has been grossly disproportionate" (emphasis added)); United States v. Feldman, 853 F.2d 648, 664 (9th Cir. 1988) (evaluating for excessiveness a forfeiture of nearly $2 million along with five years of probation on mail fraud conviction, concurrent sentences of 10 years for RICO violations and interstate transportation of fraudulently obtained funds), cert. denied, 489 U.S. 1030 (1989); United States v. Littlefield, 821 F.2d 1365, 1368 (9th Cir. 1987) (noting that the court must determine that the forfeiture of the entire property "together with other punishments imposed is not so disproportionate to the offense committed as to violate the

Darley surveyed several hundred non lawyer respondents who assigned longer penalties for two crimes than for one but did not double the sentence. The authors refer to this as the "multiple-offense discount notion."

Eighth Amendment challenges are also combining state and federal penalties, implicitly acknowledging that the Eighth Amendment limits the totality of punishment imposed by all governments. A similar trend is emerging in cases involving due process challenges to multiple punitive damage awards. Unable to limit punitive damages between private parties using the Eighth Amendment, courts are beginning to employ the Due Process Clause to perform the same function, limiting the totality of cumulated penalties.

Constitution"); United States v. Busher, 817 F.2d 1409, 1415 n.10, 1416 (9th Cir. 1987) (ordering the district court to assess the total penalty, including forfeiture, jail time, and fines, to determine whether the combined penalty exceeds constitutional limits and to limit either the forfeiture or the other penalties if it does). "' For example, one trial judge relied on the dual sovereignty exception to double jeopardy to reject the defendants' double jeopardy challenge to their federal prosecution after state forfeiture proceedings, but went on to note: Defendants also contend that this criminal prosecution constitutes an excessive punishment which violates the Eighth Amendment even if it is not prohibited by the Double Jeopardy Clause. Based on the present record I am unable to conclude that the forfeitures in this case were so excessive as to bar any further punishment through criminal prosecution. United States v. Collins, 877 F. Supp. 516, 519 n.2 (D. Or. 1995); see also United States v. 429 S. Main St., 843 F. Supp. 337, 342 (S.D. Ohio 1993) (rejecting excessive fines challenge to federal civil forfeiture of home after state conviction, considering "combined penalty" of forfeiture and state sentence of one year and fine of $6000 for three drug sales), aff'd in part, 52 F.3d 1416 (6th Cir. 1995).

These judges understand that punishment which may not be excessive alone may become excessive if repeated. It is time this intuition became a routine ingredient of the constitutional review of punishment.

CONCLUSION

Federal and state courts have the constitutional duty to ensure that persons are not subjected to cruel and unusual punishment under ICCPR and laws of the United States. Time has come for courts to take a fresh look into how Arizona operates. Arizona cannot be allowed to continue with the practices it has to date because the Arizona Supreme Court and federal courts refuse to perform their duties.

Books have the POWER to change lives!

Best Selection of Books, Newspapers & Magazines to Inmates.
Serving Correctional Facilitys since 1990

Order our New Catalog $12.95

We have made depositing funds to your account, much easier for your family and friends. By adding funds, you can make purchases for products whenever you choose with your credit. With this purchase we will forward you a deposit confirmation, stating that you have funds available in your account with a message from the sender. These funds are available immediately for use. www.sureshotbooks.com Then you can place orders via e-mail.

E-mail Us at info@sureshotbooks.com
on: SmartJailMail - JPay - Corrlinks - Getting Out -
ConnectNetwork - Access Corrections - Securus

Faster Service **www.sureshotbooks.com**

Here at SureShot Books, our goal is to provide reasonably priced Books, Newspapers & Magazines

Books have the POWER to change lives

THE LATEST MAGAZINE & NEWPAPER SUBSCRIPTIONS

Order our New Catalog $12.95

We have made depositing funds to your account, much easier for your family and friends. By adding funds, you can make purchases for products whenever you choose with your credit. With this purchase we will forward you a deposit confirmation, stating that you have funds available in your account with a message from the sender. These funds are available immediately for use. www.sureshotbooks.com Then you can place orders via e-mail.

E-mail Us at info@sureshotbooks.com
on: SmartJailMail - JPay - Corrlinks - Getting Out - ConnectNetwork - Access Corrections - Securus

Books have the POWER to change lives

Favorites from SureShot Books Publishing LLC acclaimed authors

Our Authors give a NEW revelation to story telling & facts without rival.

Need more info on our large selection have love one's visit us at
www.sureshotbooks.com

www.ingramcontent.com/pod-product-compliance
Lightning Source LLC
Chambersburg PA
CBHW051536020426
42333CB00016B/1962